How to Make and Use
visual aids

Nicola Harford and Nicola Baird

Heinemann Educational Publishers
Halley Court, Jordan Hill, Oxford OX2 8EJ
A Division of Reed Educational & Professional Publishing Ltd

Heinemann Educational Botswana (Publishers) (Pty) Ltd
PO Box 10103, Village Post Office, Gaborone, Botswana

Jhango Heinemann
PO Box 1259, Blantyre, Malawi

Heinemann Publishers (Pty) Limited
PO Box 781940, Sandton 2146, Johannesburg, South Africa

OXFORD   MELBOURNE   AUCKLAND
JOHANNESBURG   BLANTYRE   GABORONE
IBADAN   PORTSMOUTH (NH) USA   CHICAGO

First published by Heinemann Educational Publishers in 1997

British Library Cataloguing in Publication Data
A catalogue record for this book is available from the British Library.

Cover illustration by Sarah John
Illustrations in text by Sarah John
Text designed by Susan Clarke, Reading, Berkshire
ISBN 0 435 92317 X

Phototypeset by Roger Stevens, Reading, Berkshire
Printed and bound in Great Britain by The Bath Press, Bath

00 01 02 10 9 8 7 6 5

Contents

Introduction

School teachers, teacher trainers and development workers know that visual aids help people to learn and remember, but when time is short and resources few, visual aids may seem to be a luxury they cannot afford.

This book shows that you can make visual aids quickly and easily, using low-cost materials which are simple to find or improvise, wherever you are in the world. All the techniques described in this book have been adapted and developed by VSO volunteers and their national colleagues, working in schools and development projects throughout Africa, Asia, the Caribbean and the Pacific. *How to Make and Use Visual Aids* draws together know-how and tips from this first-hand experience in situations where resources are limited.

The book is designed to be used by teachers, teacher trainers and development workers from any skill background. *How to Make and Use Visual Aids* can readily be used by people with little or no experience of making or using visual aids. It can also extend the range and ambition of experienced users by providing them with ideas, practical tips and new ways of thinking about visual aids.

Why make your own visual aids?

Making your own visual aids has many advantages:

► it is less expensive than buying ready-made visual aids – even if they are available – or employing an artist to make them

► you can choose visual aids which are directly relevant and appropriate to your local community

► you can design your visual aid specifically to suit your resources, your purposes and your students' or learners' needs

► planning a visual aid will help you to define your teaching or training objectives and to clarify in your own mind what it is you are trying to communicate

► students and adult learners can work with you in planning, designing and making the visual aids.

How to use this book

How to Make and Use Visual Aids is divided into six chapters:

► **Chapter 1: Guidelines for making visual aids** covers choosing and planning which visual aid to make, according to the type of lesson or activity you are involved in. It discusses methods of pre-testing and evaluating the visual aids, and gives some general advice on preparing for your lesson, extension session or workshop.

► **Chapter 2: Re-usable visual aids which carry information.** These are objects used to carry information. They involve construction rather than design skills and can be used over and over again, conveying different information each time, such as chalkboards.

► **Chapter 3: Visual aids which display information.** These are displays of information which are made more effective by using simple graphic design techniques, such as posters.

► **Chapter 4: Visual aids which summarise complex information.** These are visual summaries of complex information, such as charts and graphs.

► **Chapter 5: Visual aids for activities.** These are visual aids which are part of learning activities, such as masks in role-play.

► **Chapter 6: Basic techniques and materials** describes simple drawing and lettering techniques and gives detailed instructions for making and improvising resources such as chalk, glue and papier mâché.

The visual aids in this book have been grouped in Chapters 2–5 according to their main common characteristics. Each of these chapters provides practical advice and step-by-step instructions for making visual aids. In each chapter the visual aids are organised so that the most common aids are described first, and those which are more unusual are given later. You may like to move on to the more complex ones once you have mastered the basic techniques and increased your level of skill and confidence.

To decide which visual aid is the most appropriate for your purpose, first read through Chapter 1. Then consult the contents page and the introductions to Chapters 2–5. Where you need to use basic techniques, these are explained in Chapter 6.

The section on **Useful contacts** on page 119 lists organisations around the world which you can contact for advice, free material or catalogues.

Make use of local knowledge

You can build on the advice given in this book by finding out about local techniques for making things: ask carpenters, potters, craft workers and others for help and advice. You may need to ask them to help you to find suitable wood, clay or other materials, or to give you advice if things do not work out as you had planned. Try to use recycled timber, or wood cut from well-managed woodlands.

Discovery and participatory approaches

This is primarily a practical resource book. The background to discovery methods in education and participatory approaches in development work is treated only very briefly here.

The 'chalk and talk' method of teaching curriculum subjects, where the teacher talks and the students listen, is gradually being changed to 'learning by doing' or discovery methods. In discovery methods, the teacher creates opportunities for the students to find out knowledge for themselves through, for example, project work, doing experiments, and so on.

Throughout this book it is assumed that teachers and teacher trainers will involve their students in the making of the visual aids. In doing this the students will learn and remember more.

In a similar way this book encourages community and development workers to use visual aids as tools to enable local people to share information, make their own analysis of a situation and plans for action, and take responsibility for decision-making. This is known as the participatory approach. It aims to involve local people at every stage of the activity. Participatory approaches which have a high degree of listening and learning can involve outsiders handing over control to local people.

In using participatory approaches, the development worker has to find a balance between learning rapidly and avoiding bias, on the one hand; and losing precision and standardisation of information that other techniques might provide, on the other. Many participatory methods use visual aids which are made by or with members of the community.

Safety

Knives, saws and other tools can be dangerous if they are not handled properly. Some glues, paints, dyes and other chemicals may be poisonous. Be sure to use and store them carefully, and keep them out of the reach of children. In schools, teachers must use their professional judgement in deciding whether children are old enough to use cutting tools, such as scissors, glues and other substances which are harmful if swallowed, or processes such as boiling water, which may be dangerous. Teachers will also need to decide upon the level of supervision needed by children of different ages.

 You will see this symbol wherever special care needs to be taken.

While all the material in this book has been carefully assessed, neither VSO nor Heinemann Publishers can accept liability for accidents of any kind.

1

Guidelines for making visual aids

Choosing the appropriate visual aid

There are a number of issues to think about carefully before starting to make a visual aid:

▶ Can you involve the students in making the visual aid? The students can then use their imagination and knowledge to think through problems and find out answers for themselves.

▶ Can you bring in the real object instead of drawing the object on the board?

▶ Can you use local cheap materials?

▶ Are there any commercially-produced visual aids that would be useful? Are they suitable for the students' needs?

▶ Can the visual aid be made simply?

What kind of activity?

Before you make a visual aid, you need to decide which of the following categories your activity fits into: teaching, or training, or project work with communities. There is of necessity some overlap between them, so you may find that your work falls into more than one category.

Teaching

Trained teachers will be familiar with different teaching methods and different types of visual aid. However, both new and experienced teachers can gain from new ideas for stimulating their students' interest and learning.

Making visual aids with your students can bring learning to life. Students can be given the opportunity to examine carefully the topic or theme they are studying through making, for example, masks for a play about immunisation. They can ask questions about points they do not understand and so come to understand the issue thoroughly.

Learning takes place most effectively when students take part in the process: doing, making and finding out things for themselves. In this way they remember the facts and attitudes far longer and more clearly.

Training

In this book, 'training' is used to describe the transfer of knowledge or skills to adults, unlike school situations where the learners are children or adolescents. Training tends to focus on job skills or raising awareness about important issues. The settings and techniques for training range from formal to very informal. If the trainees are employed in the formal sector, for example in-service training for government workers, the training techniques are likely to be quite formal and take place, perhaps, in a training centre with electricity and other facilities. If the trainees generate their own income or the training is unrelated to job skills, for example farmers or a group of young mothers, the setting and techniques are likely to be much more informal, and take place in an open field or village meeting place.

There are two approaches to training:

▶ *conventional training where the trainer decides what to teach and what the trainees learn.* Individual changes in behaviour based on the 'taught' knowledge lead to improvements in the way individuals carry out their jobs.

▶ *learner-centred strategies where learners identify needs, set goals and learn for themselves.* Here trainers are, in essence, facilitators. This people-oriented, participatory approach has now become widespread. These methods are a response to the need for 'process-oriented' training, which occurs when the objectives are varied or complex. They are useful for provoking a change in attitudes, knowledge and skills.

A more participatory approach to training

Situations usually lie somewhere between the fully conventional and the fully participatory. The style adopted will necessarily have consequences for the type of visual aid chosen and its purpose.

Project work with communities: appraisal, planning, monitoring and evaluation

There has been an increasing use of participatory techniques in project work with communities. Here, visual aids can be used as part of a range of participatory and people-centred methods to allow clear communication between outsiders/development workers and local people.

A more conventional approach to training

Visual aids can be used in a participatory approach at all stages of a development project or programme. Participatory methods enable the community and development workers to share information and decisions on what needs to be done, how it should be done, how to decide what is effective and to assess whether it has been successful.

Visual aids enable non-literate people to analyse, express and record their choices. Communication is effected not only with diagrams which are intended to explain, but also with pictures which represent reality. For example, in a village in North West Pakistan, posters were produced showing different water supply options and the related costs. The villagers were then able to choose the level of service they preferred (planning). In a second example, in a chicken-rearing project in Indonesia non-literate women ticked pictures in a booklet to show when and how many eggs were laid, and how many chicks eventually hatched (monitoring).

What are you trying to communicate?

After defining the activity, the next step is to ask yourself what it is that you are trying to communicate. What is your aim?

The visual aid which is most appropriate to your situation depends upon what you want to teach. For example, if you teach academic subjects in a secondary school you may choose to make maps, bar charts, and so on. Mathematics teachers are usually familiar with classroom displays of two- or three-dimensional geometric shapes. Language teachers may use puppets for drama and role-play. If you are teaching technical subjects or training people to do a job, you may need to teach manual skills with real objects, or with models in simulations or demonstrations, for example, using a papier mâché model of a goat to show how to kill the animal humanely.

Who are the visual aids for?

Before choosing the appropriate visual aid and drawing the first version, you need to consider the following questions:

▶ Are the students/learners visually literate? Are they familiar with the process of finding out information from pictures and symbols? Can they understand them?

   Research has shown that many people are not used to interpreting pictures, especially in countries with low literacy rates. You can find out what can and does work by talking to other teachers and development workers with experience of using visual aids locally. Spend time with the students before introducing visual aids. This establishes a relationship and builds up trust.

▶ Have the learners had any formal education?

Even those who have attended school for some years may not have seen many pictures.

▶ What language should any words be written in?

If the students are making the visual aid themselves, they can decide which language is best to use. However, in groups where some members cannot read, words may not be appropriate.

There may be political considerations involved in the choice of language. For example, if one group of people feels marginalised within the country, choosing the official, national language for a poster may alienate them from the message. On the other hand, if the topic is in some way thought of as official, the national language of the country may be chosen, rather than the local language.

In all cases choose simple words and phrases. Texts should always be written directly in a language and not translated, because a translation may convey a meaning that was not intended.

▶ Do specific colours have any special significance for the students/learners?

Certain colours have different meanings in different cultures, so it is important to find out if there are particular associations for a colour, for example are mourning clothes traditionally white? Again ask teachers and/or colleagues. However, black and white pictures are very clear and effective on posters and wallcharts.

▶ What social, cultural and religious beliefs and practices need to be taken into account when designing and planning the visual aids?

There will be instances when visual aids need to convey issues that are sensitive, threatening or embarrassing. Building up trust and minimising the possibility of causing offence in these cases is important. At times it may be preferable for the subject to be introduced by someone of the same community and sex.

▶ What other characteristics need to be taken into account?

To be effective you need to take the gender, age, class, caste and ethnic characteristics of the students into account – the differences as well as the similarities. You need to be aware of the roles of men and women and examine the responsibilities of the varying age groups. For example, if younger women are generally responsible for pounding grain, then to have a poster showing a man or old woman doing this may not be as effective. Information about some beliefs and practices may be difficult to discover before choosing and pre-testing the visual aid. It is important that the visual aid reflects the current and particular situation.

▶ How do students or local people obtain information and communicate?

❝ Anything to do with birth, including discussing it, was thought of as women's business. We had been offered some flashcards to be used by traditional birth attendants (TBAs). But some of our TBA trainers were unwilling to use these flashcards in certain rural areas, worrying that they might be left lying around the village and worse, seen by children. ❞
Community health co-ordinator, Bangladesh

To answer this question another question must be asked: Which visual aids have credibility and for which purposes, at present? With this knowledge, you can then build on what is familiar to the students/learners. If you want to create an impact use something unfamiliar, such as a magnet board, or use a familiar technique in an unfamiliar way, for example traditional drama can be used in training to explore different attitudes.

▶ How relevant to the students is the situation or issue you wish to show?

If the students/learners feel the people in a picture are from a different place, and are therefore 'strangers', they will feel that the 'problem' portrayed in the picture has nothing to do with their lives. They may not, therefore, want to learn about it or find a solution to it.

The visual aid must show situations that students/learners can relate to, using images from their own lives.

▶ How familiar are the students/learners with the subject of the proposed visual aid?

You need to find out what existing knowledge, attitudes and practices the students/learners have regarding the subject matter before building on the topic or introducing it.

▶ Are the necessary resources available?

You will need to know whether the necessary resources are available to support change in habits or traditional ways in the school or community, particularly in the long-term. These resources include materials, money and skills, as well as support from community elders, leaders and politicians.

These questions are crucial to avoid making mistakes when designing and using visual aids.

Practical considerations

When you have decided on the aim and the appropriate activity, there are a number of factors which will determine your choice of visual aid:

▶ Does it need to be made quickly, for example in less than an hour? Check how long it will take to make. Is there time for follow-up, or will the visual aid be useful without further teaching, training or facilitation?

▶ Does it need to be re-usable? Will it be handled repeatedly and therefore need to be durable? Will it be on permanent display and/or need to be able to withstand the elements?

▶ Does it need to be easy to transport? What transport is available? Will it have to be carried on foot?

▶ Where will it be used – in a classroom, clinic or government office, in a village meeting place or in the fields on a community project?

As well as time, already mentioned above, an approximate estimate of money and other resources will be required at this stage. Check what materials you require and find out what is available. Is there a budget with which to buy materials, or is there a stock available? Do multiple copies need to be made? Can this be done cheaply and quickly by using resources available locally (for example, jelly copier, photocopier, carbon paper or banda – see pages 102–103).

Practice version of the proposed visual aid

Make a rough or practice version of the visual aid. For any two-dimensional visual aid, for example, a picture or a map, make a quick sketch in pencil. For a three-dimensional visual aid, for example a model, make it using thin paper or card. Where the technique is unfamiliar (for example, papier mâché), experiment well in advance. It may be useful to make several versions to see which style is best. Experience shows that the practice version should be as detailed and complete as possible.

Tips for making visual aids

▶ Visual aids should be clear. Do not overcrowd the poster or board with too many pictures or words.

▶ Keep pictures as simple as possible. This makes it easier for the students/learners to see and understand; but do show enough detail for the picture to be recognisable.

▶ A picture is better understood when it has one clear meaning. Use a series of pictures to explain more than one thing or a sequence of events.

▶ Illustrate a person's whole body and not just a part of it. If only a part of a body is shown (for example, a head or hand) the picture may not be easy to understand.

▶ Pictures will be more successful if they are based on what is familiar locally – faces, clothes, houses, utensils, and so on.

▶ Food, animals and objects (like a spoon or a pot) are more difficult to recognise than pictures of people. Draw them clearly.

▶ Leave out backgrounds as these draw attention away from the message (what you want to say).

▶ Avoid making very small objects or animals too big. For example, if you show a picture of a very big mosquito people may not recognise it as the tiny insect they know.

A simple poster

► Perspective, for example a house seen in the distance, can often be very difficult to recognise.

► Symbols such as crosses, arrows, lines showing movement, skull and crossbones for danger are culturally-specific and can therefore be difficult to understand.

For more information on how to draw people, faces and objects, see Drawing, Chapter 6, pages 104–107.

Pre-testing

Pre-testing is the process of trying out a draft copy of the visual aid before the lesson or training session. It involves asking the students or interviewing a few members of the community about their reactions to the visual aid before it is produced in its final form. Not all the aids in Chapters 2 to 5 can be pre-tested, either because they will be made with the students/learners during a lesson or workshop or because they are a means of displaying ready-made items, for example a zigzag board.

Why do you need to pre-test?

The main reason for pre-testing is to gain feedback to help the teacher or development worker to make visual aids that are clearly understood by the students/learners.

It is crucial for visual aids to be pre-tested to ensure that the message cannot be misinterpreted. If a visual aid is misunderstood there may be negative or even disastrous consequences. For example, if a poster showing how to make Oral Rehydration Solution (sugar/salt solution) is misunderstood, a child may become dehydrated and die.

Not only can mistakes sometimes be harmful, they can also waste time, money and resources. Pre-testing leads to better communication and results in visual aids that are more appropriate to communities.

❝ We were sent some AIDS awareness posters which said 'Sex can kill'. We didn't ever use them because they weren't at all helpful and the message was not clear. The writing was in English and although a few people could read it, the slogan just compounded the confusion. The main image was a silhouette of a crowd scene and even I didn't understand what it meant! There was no way someone non-literate could have got anything from that poster. ❞
Graphic designer, Namibia

Pre-testing also provides feedback about whether people understand a message straightaway or whether it confuses them. You can find out whether people understand pictures in a series – do they connect them with each other, or do they interpret each one separately?

❝ We wanted to prevent deafness so (we) decided to make two posters. Each poster was divided into four pictures. They were locally drawn, produced in Nepali script and looked really nice. To pre-test we showed them to one woman and it was obvious she was confused. She couldn't see the division in the big picture – she saw just one picture so couldn't get any meaning from it. The lesson we learned was to do more pre-testing and to decide at the earliest possible stage who your audience is. ❞
Speech therapist, Nepal

How do you pre-test?
Pre-testing involves asking questions and listening to and noting down the answers. The simplest method of pre-testing is to carry out individual interviews using a questionnaire.

Preparing the questionnaire
Decide what you want to find out about each visual aid. The kind of effect it is intended to have will determine the questions you ask. Usually the questions will be open-ended, for example 'What do you see in this picture?'

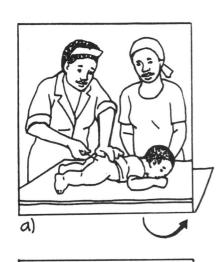

a)

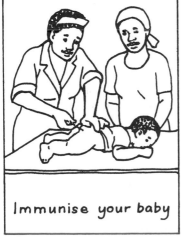

Immunise your baby

b)

Example questionnaire
This questionnaire is for guidance only as it will need to be adapted to meet specific situations.

1 What does this picture show? (Point to different parts of the picture if necessary.) For a model or three-dimensional object, ask what it looks like.

2 What does the picture mean? Is it telling you anything? If yes, what?

3 What do you like or dislike about it?

4 Is there anything in the picture which is unclear? If yes, what?

5 What would you change
  a to make it more easily understood?
  b for it to be acceptable?

6 Is there anything missing from the picture? If yes, what?

Pre-testing written text should be done separately. For example, hide the words on a poster (see (a) left) while the person looks at the picture. Then uncover the words (see (b) left) and ask the person to read the words aloud. Ask the following questions:

7 What do these words mean to you?

8 Do the words match the picture? If not, ask what words would be better, or what the picture should look like to match the words.

Keep a record of the pre-testing results – see the example over the page.

PRE-TESTING FORM				Type and title of visual aid: Poster "Immunise your baby" Date: 10/9/96 Place: Muruka						
PERSONAL INFORMATION						PICTURE			TEXT	
Age	Sex	Single or married	Years of school	Income group*	Tribe, ethnic group or caste	What do you see?	What do you dislike?	What would you change or add?	What do the words mean to you?	What would you change or add?
18	F M		6	concrete house + land	Kikuyu	✓ **	mother wearing poor clothes	better clothes for mother	✓	add: "For better health"
27	F M		2	mud house little land	Kikuyu	nurse and baby	doesn't look like clinic	make clinic look like local one	X cannot understand	

* Select 1 or 2 criteria to distinguish between rich, less rich, average, poor etc

** Correct answer: mother with a nurse who is vaccinating her baby at the clinic

Who to pre-test visual aids with

Visual aids that are to be used on their own with no teacher or development worker to explain the message should be pre-tested rigorously. However, if a simple visual aid is devised to help explain a concept with back-up from a teacher or trainer, pre-testing may be quick and informal. Where possible, pre-tests of visual aids for use with groups who have low literacy levels or are unfamiliar with visual learning should be conducted with individuals. The individuals should be representative of the students or groups you are going to work with and different from people you have consulted before making the first draft copy.

❝ I always bounced ideas off my counterparts. What seemed to work well was if I pitched the message, for example on a poster, at the audience's level, and then asked my counterparts to take the rough edges off it. But it was at least a year into my posting before they felt comfortable enough to tell me, 'You can't do that!' Until you have a good appreciation of your colleagues' culture and language people tend to say, 'Yes, that's nice'. ❞
Environmental educator, Thailand

Make sure that pre-testing is carried out with people who are the least likely to understand the visual aid (poorest, least exposure to visual aids, least educated) and who will benefit most from an appropriate visual aid. The number of people you ask in a pre-test depends on how long it takes for a consistent trend to emerge in your findings.

Getting the most out of the pre-test

Ask people in advance if they agree to being involved with the pre-testing. Explain that you are asking for their opinion and advice and that you are not testing their knowledge. Remember not to test more than ten pictures at a time and do not give your opinion, or smile/frown while the person is giving their opinion on the visual aid.

Analysing the pre-test results

The way you analyse the pre-test results depends on how many people you pre-tested and whether the visual aid was simple (a single poster) or more complicated (a series of flashcards or a short puppet play). For each picture, go through your pre-testing form(s) and note how many people could identify and understand the picture and the text. As a rough guide, if the majority of the people (three-quarters or more) like and understand the poster you only need to make a few changes. If less than a third like and understand it, you may have to re-think your ideas completely. You may also want to see if people with certain opinions are of any particular age, income or ethnic group. That may explain their response. Put similar remarks together. For example, how many people said the clothing was wrong or the baby looked ill? Put together similar suggestions people made about adding to or changing the picture. Then decide which comments and suggestions are repeated frequently. Use these comments to make the changes in the visual aid.

Some visual aids will need pre-testing and revising several times before a suitable version is found.

It is very important to pre-test your initial design, and then, after you've gone back to the drawing board, to re-test the improved version. If the message is not succeeding then you must start again.
Nutritionist, Zambia

Producing a final version of the visual aid

Assemble everything you need before you start. If students or learners are helping you, discuss with them what each person should do.

Read Chapters 2–5 for details of how to make specific visual aids, and Chapter 6 for some basic techniques, such as drawing people, lettering, making chalk, glue and papier mâché.

Monitoring and evaluating the visual aids

Keep a record of how, when, where and with whom a visual aid is used both during pre-testing and when using the final version. Note how many copies are made, where they are stored and their condition. Keep a record of any problems you had with making or using the visual aid.

Evaluating visual aids means measuring the success or failure of a visual aid. Did it communicate what was intended? Ask for feedback from the students. If you do this, mistakes can be avoided in the future, time and effort will be saved and the students and community will be better served.

Using your visual aids effectively

Here are some general rules which apply in most cases.

Prepare for the activity in advance

▶ Spend time planning the lesson, training session or workshop where a visual aid is to be used or produced.

▶ Prepare the physical environment too. Chairs or mats should be set out so everyone can work together and/or easily see the visual aid displayed.

▶ Ensure that there will be no distraction from noise or other interruptions.

Prepare yourself

▶ Practise speaking and using the visual aid separately, and then speaking and using it at the same time. Either use a mirror and stand in front of it, or ask a friend to be the 'audience'.

▶ Be aware of your body language and gestures. Ask a friend to notice what you do with your hands while you are speaking. Some gestures can be very distracting.

▶ Some gestures are culturally unacceptable, for example, pointing with your toes is very impolite in some cultures. Eye contact is very important in European culture as it helps to include the students or participants. However, in China for example eye contact is considered rude.

▶ Be aware of your and others' behaviour in relation to the opposite sex. For example, if a woman is in a position of authority, as a teacher or facilitator, some men may find this threatening.

▶ A mixed group of men and women will behave differently from a single sex group. The age of the students or trainees will also affect their relationship with the teacher or development worker, whether they are all the same age or of varying ages.

▶ Be aware of your choice of language level. It should be clear and direct, neither confusing nor talking down to the listeners. Avoid jargon.

Getting started

▶ When you are using a small picture, give everyone time to look at it before going on to the next point.

▶ Diagrams should be simple. Make sure people look at the picture of the whole item before focusing on the detail.

▶ When showing a picture in a lecture, give people sufficient time to look at it.

- When showing a series of pictures make sure the order is understood, especially if the local written script is read from right to left.

- Any visual aid being shown must coincide with the words being spoken at that time. It should then be put aside as the discussion moves on.

- There is no need to provide a picture for each part of the lesson or workshop.

After the session

- Decide whether to store or display the visual aid. When storing, take account of the damage strong sunlight, humidity and insects do to visual aids. They need suitable protection.

- If the visual aid is being left with the community, keep a record of it (a photograph or sketch) so that you can refer to it again.

- Respond to requests for copies wherever possible.

The guidelines in this chapter will help you to prepare and use your visual aid effectively with your students or group. Chapters 2–5 list visual aids with step-by-step information on how to make and use them.

2

Re-usable visual aids which carry information

This chapter describes visual aids which can be used over and over again, conveying different information each time. To make them, you need to follow the basic, step-by-step instructions which are given for each one.

Remember that the visual aids which are most commonly used and simplest to make are described first. If you would like to be more ambitious, but are concerned that your choice of visual aid is beyond your scope, ask the art and crafts teacher or local crafts workers to give you advice or help.

All the visual aids in this chapter can be used in a variety of situations, indoors or outdoors, with children, students or adult learners, literate or non-literate participants. They can all be used with large or small groups. Zigzag multiboards may be the least suitable for using with groups of more than ten, but this depends on the size of the boards. Wall displays, whiteboards and washing-line displays are the quickest to make, but also the least durable. You will need to have special pens to use a whiteboard.

If you need to travel with your visual aid, you will find that zigzag multiboards, rope and pole displays, washing-line displays and some of the display boards described are the easiest to transport.

Chalkboard

One of the most useful and most commonly used visual aids in teaching is the chalkboard. It is a board with a smooth surface, usually painted black or dark green, for writing on with chalk. For many schools in the world a chalkboard is the main teaching resource.

A chalkboard can be:
▶ fixed permanently to an inside or outside wall
▶ portable – mounted on a stand or easel, possibly with castors attached to the legs, so it can be moved easily around a room or taken outside, or made of canvas so that it can be rolled up. In some countries ready-made mobile chalkboards are available which can be rolled up.

In some areas of the world, the end of a building is used as a chalkboard:
▶ to help the public who pass it to maintain their literacy
▶ to share learning messages
▶ to provide information on local events.

This method of public communication is particularly popular in China and around the Pacific.

How to use a chalkboard

Always ask if everyone in the room can see the chalkboard clearly, and tell them to let you know if they cannot (for example, because of sunlight, their view is blocked, and so on).

The 'chalk and talk' method of teaching and training can be limited if every session becomes a lecture and there is little interaction with the learners. Try to have some eye contact with the students, rather than looking at the board when you are speaking or listening to them.

To use a chalkboard successfully for teaching or development work, it is important to develop your chalkboard technique. Here are three points to help you:

❝ It took me ages to develop the knack of writing on a chalkboard without breaking the chalk. **❞**
Business adviser, Kenya

▶ Always write clearly. It is important to remember that it takes a great deal of practice to learn to write legibly on a chalkboard. (See Lettering, Chapter 6, pages 109–110.)

▶ Draw simply. Do not include any unnecessary details. If you have to draw maps or diagrams on the board, draw them before class or the training session: you could use a template (see Templates, Chapter 6, pages 117–118). If you have to draw during class, draw quickly. Ask the students questions about the picture to keep their attention.

▶ Plan the layout of the chalkboard. Before you begin your lesson or training session, draw exactly what you are going to write/draw on the chalkboard in your notebook. For example, for a science lesson:

   – Draw two vertical lines from the top of the board to the bottom. The board is now divided into three separate areas as shown below.

Which of these conducts electricity?	Guess	Result

   – Draw a large H on the chalkboard. You have divided the chalkboard into four separate areas. In one part you can write questions on a text, in another the answers, then new words. Finally write the homework. See the example on the left.

Questions	Answers	Homework
1. Who ran through the forest after the hare?	1.	Write your own story with a message about two animals.
	New words tortoise web trap	

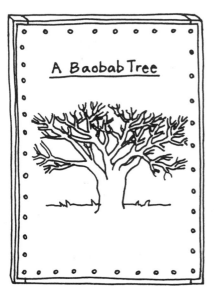

How to make a portable chalkboard

You will need
- a piece of linoleum, plywood, canvas or other light, stiff material, approximately 65 cm × 1 m
- sandpaper
- black paint or special chalkboard paint (see Chapter 6, page 101 for instructions on making your own chalkboard paint)
- lengths of timber to make a frame (optional)

What you need to do
1 Choose your material.

2 If you are using linoleum or plywood, sand one side of it to an even roughness.

3 Paint the roughened surface.

4 When it is dry, paint it again.

5 To prevent the board from warping, make a wooden frame and nail the board to it.

This chalkboard is easy to carry, but it could also be fixed to a wall or stood on an easel with castors.

How to make a cloth chalkboard

This is light and easy to carry. It can be used with groups of up to ten people.

You will need
- a piece of oil cloth or a smooth, thick piece of cotton cloth, about 65 cm × 1 m
- a round wooden pole or stick (dowelling is ideal), slightly longer than the long side of the cloth
- a length of cord slightly longer than the stick or pole
- a can of matt black paint
- sandpaper
- glue
- nails

What you need to do

1 Roughen the shiny side of the oil cloth with the sandpaper. If you are using cotton cloth, apply a thin coat of glue to one side and leave it to dry.

2 Apply two coats of black paint to the oil cloth or cotton cloth, allowing the first coat to dry completely before applying the second coat.

3 When the paint is dry, glue or nail the pole to one of the long sides of the cloth.

4 Attach a piece of cord to each end of the pole so that the chalkboard can be hung on a nail.

When you roll up the chalkboard, make sure the painted surface is rolled inside.

How to make a fixed chalkboard

A traditional, fixed chalkboard needs to be durable and big enough to be used with large groups. Make this only if you are experienced at working with cement. You will need someone to help you move it as it will be very heavy.

You will need
- ► four lengths of timber to make a frame, at least 1 m × 1.5 m (or whatever size you want the board to be)
- ► nails
- ► wire mesh
- ► a trowel or builder's float
- ► concrete mix and water
- ► chalkboard paint (see Chapter 6, page 101)

What you need to do

1 Make a timber frame about 1 m × 1.5 m, and stretch the wire mesh across it. Fix the mesh in position using the nails.

2 Mix the concrete mix to a consistency that is neither too wet nor too stiff.

3 Pack the concrete mix firmly into the wire mesh, and create a flat surface by smoothing it with a trowel or float. Then, if you can, cover it with damp cloth or sacking. (This should not touch the surface of the concrete.)

4 Allow the mixture to become firm to the touch (an hour or two), smoothing out any trowel marks as it becomes firmer. It is best for concrete to set slowly and evenly. To help this, once it is firm to the touch, you can damp it down occasionally with water. You can use a watering can, or a bucket with holes punched in the bottom. Allow a little water to run over the surface. If it leaves any marks on the concrete, smooth them out immediately with a trowel. It will take about two days to dry completely.

6 My students made a chalkboard but it was too heavy to carry around and tended to crack because we hadn't enough water to be able to damp down the cement thoroughly when it was 'setting'. 9
Building instructor, Kenya

5 When it is completely dry, paint the board with chalkboard paint.

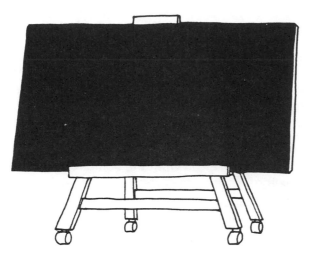

6 The board can be fixed permanently to a wall inside the classroom using nails or screws; or it can be mounted on a stand or easel. If the board needs to be moved around, then castors (small wheels) can be put on the legs of the stand. Take care: the easel needs to be strong enough to support the board. Get someone to help when you move the easel.

When the chalkboard is dry, be careful how you move it as it will be very heavy, and there is always a risk that it may crack. Be sure to secure it so that it will not fall over and injure anyone.

Tips on using and caring for your chalkboard

▶ Before using your chalkboard, rub a chalky cloth or duster over it. This will make it easier to write on.

▶ If your chalkboard is old or is very greasy, you could wash it. However, it would be better to repaint it.

▶ If you clean the board with downward strokes, there is far less chalk dust.

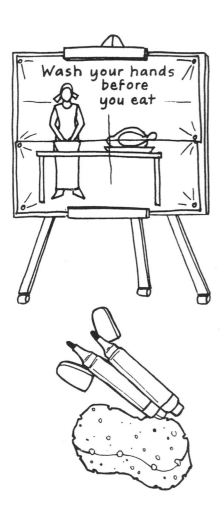

Whiteboard

A whiteboard has a smooth shiny white surface which can be written on with special pens and wiped clean with a dry cloth. Commercially available whiteboards are designed to be either:
▶ screwed to a wall permanently, or
▶ free-standing boards with legs and castors.

Whiteboards are good visual aids for teaching and training and they are easier to write on than chalkboards.

How to make a whiteboard

You will need
▶ one or more thick, white plastic bags
▶ a piece of thick cardboard or thin timber
▶ drawing pins or tacks

What you need to do
1 Cut open one or more white plastic bags.

2 Stretch them over a piece of thick cardboard or thin timber, with the inside of the bags facing outwards.

3 Use the drawing pins or tacks to fix the plastic securely.

How to use a whiteboard

You will need
- ▶ special thick whiteboard pens which have washable ink
- ▶ a sponge or cloth to clean the board

Providing you have the special pens you can use many different surfaces, for example, plastic sheeting, sticky-back plastic and so on. Do not allow young children to play with the plastic bags – they could put them over their heads and suffocate.

Experiment with different coloured pens on whiteboards – some colours are more difficult to read, such as red. Do use the correct pens because normal felt-tip pens leave permanent marks on the board.

If you have a portable chalkboard, one side could be used as a whiteboard.

Whiteboards can be used in the same way as chalkboards for writing or drawing. In the beginning it may be difficult to keep the writing horizontal, and the same size and style, so you will need to practise. (See Lettering, Chapter 6, page 109–111.)

Before writing on the whiteboard in your lesson or session, draw the summary in the lesson plan. It needs to be clear and well-arranged.

Bar charts, line graphs, pie charts and diagrams (see pages 67–73) can be drawn on the whiteboard before a maths or geography lesson.

❝ I found it great to teach young children more English. Every lesson I put different letters in a slot, for example, C. Then next to them I put up pictures which started with the letter – cup, cat, crocodile. ❞
TEFL teacher, Malawi

Zigzag multiboard

A zigzag multiboard is a series of three or four rectangular boards. They are joined together along the sides by hinges so that they can be easily folded up and carried. Each board can be of a different type, for example, a whiteboard, a chalkboard, a flannelboard and so on.

The size of the boards for the zigzag multiboard depends on what you want to use them for. If you want to make a screen for the children to read behind in the classroom, each board would need to be 1 m × 1.5 m.

How to make a zigzag multiboard

The following instructions are to make three or four basic boards for a zigzag multiboard.

You will need
► strong, lightweight material that is easily available locally, for example, plywood or strong cardboard to make a board of the size you require
► cloth, glue or sticky tape for attaching the boards together
► string, rope or cloth strips to make handles
► the items necessary for the individual boards (see below)

What you need to do

1 Decide what size each board should be. This is important if you want to be able to carry the board easily. Make each board that you need, following the instructions in this chapter:
chalkboard, page 22
whiteboard, page 24
flannelboard, page 33
display board, page 29
magnet board, page 31

If you want to be able to fold the outer boards inwards when closing the multiboard, make sure that they are narrower than the two inner boards.

2 Lie the finished boards side-by-side on the ground, face down.

3 Attach the boards to each other. There are two ways of doing this:

a use strong, wide sticky tape, such as masking tape or electrician's tape to attach each board to the next, or
b cut long strips of canvas, or other strong cloth, and glue them over the joins.

Remember to leave a small space between each board so that the multiboard can be folded flat.

4 Make the handles. Using strips of cloth, attach them firmly to the reverse of the outer boards, close to where they join the inner boards.

Old belts or rubber strips can be fastened around the closed zigzag boards. Strong string attached and tied either side of the handles would also keep the boards firmly closed for carrying or storing.

Closing the multiboard

String, rope or cloth strips for the handles

String or wire with cloth strips as patches for strength

or rubber strip or belt

How to use a zigzag multiboard

You can use each part of the zigzag multiboard for a different teaching purpose, depending on the needs of your audience. It is most useful for teaching young children, but secondary school teachers and development workers will also find it useful for display purposes.

You can stand it on the floor or on a table with each board at an angle to the next (in a zigzag), so that it is both stable and eye-catching.

You can open out the zigzag board completely and stand it on the floor or hang it on a wall, or you could also close it up and use one of the boards at a time (see the examples below). In a primary school, you could place it in a corner of the classroom so that it sections off a part of it. Then, for example, students could sit and read undisturbed.

Different ways of using a zigzag multiboard

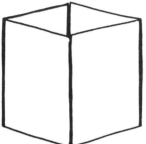

Wall display

Displaying items on a classroom wall is a well-known, tried and tested educational method. A wall display is a collection of many different types of items and materials put up on a wall to make an interesting and informative display. In a classroom, the display can consist of the students' own work; and in development work it can be used to convey information to the community.

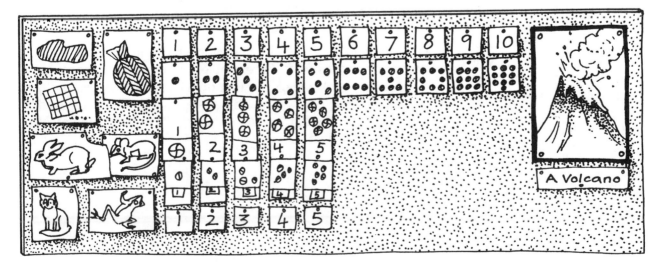

How to make a wall display

You will need

▶ either large sheets of paper, or mats, or cloth – traditional prints or large leaves are effective as background material or as a border
▶ drawing pins to pin up the display items
▶ the items for display

For information on where to obtain paper, and standard paper sizes, see Paper, Chapter 6, page 113.

There may be a variety of local materials which would be useful for wall displays. Ask your students, colleagues and local people for their suggestions.

In a classroom, the items for display may be students' own work, such as paintings or projects, and in development work it could be a selection of posters. Try to select a variety of different pieces to make the display more interesting.

What you need to do

A wall display should create an impact. It is therefore important to arrange posters and to display written material as effectively as possible. Use different coloured paper to add contrast. You can also include various shapes and textures, for example, circles cut out of cloth.

Every piece of paper should have neat straight edges; or use pinking shears to make a zigzag pattern.

Each piece of paper needs to be pinned carefully on the board. If you do not have enough drawing pins, glue two pieces of paper together. Then use two pins, one at each end.

How to use a wall display

A well-made wall display can be used for weeks in a classroom, or it can be changed every month. Students' poems together with illustrations and other creative writing can be pinned up. The class could make a wall newspaper showing their news and opinions too.

Each group in project work can decide what kind of display will best illustrate their topic. For example, one group may choose to make a scrapbook and display that on the classroom wall. Another may mount their paintings on to a piece of card and pin the card to the wall. It is important to allow the students to decide themselves on the final product.

❛ Most classrooms had nothing on the walls, maybe that's because there wasn't much wall; they were mostly window and door. Also it was hard to pin up displays to lime and clay (wattle and daub) walls. When they were pinned up they were stolen because there was no security. What we used instead was a coconut leaf mat – you could stick things onto that or hook them through the fronds. ❜
In-service teacher trainer, Zanzibar

The top class in a primary school in India were studying how newspapers were made. The trainee teacher discussed with his supervisor what follow-up activities he could do. She suggested that the students could make their own class newspaper and display it on the wall.

The trainee teacher explained to the class what they were going to do and discussed what they could put in their newspaper. He wrote all their ideas on the chalkboard. After some more discussion the students voted on the ideas and chose the best. They then divided into groups of four or five.

Each group elected a 'leader' and discussed what to write about, draw and so on. The trainee teacher acted as a facilitator, going around listening to the suggestions in the groups and giving suggestions and opinions when asked for.

Over a period of a month in their English lessons and after school, the students prepared their articles, jokes, illustrations and so on. One day the lecturer supervising the trainee noticed that occasionally he interfered with the students' discussions too much. They discussed this after the lesson and the trainee agreed to allow the students to make their own decisions.

When the class had finished their newspaper, they mounted it on paper and pinned it to the walls around the classroom.

Display board

A display board is any kind of board on which visual and written materials can be pinned or glued. It can be used to display students' work, give information about a new development activity or perhaps display instructions for operating machinery (for example, a photocopier).

6 There are all kinds of display boards, but if I was training outside and there wasn't anything solid to use, I'd sometimes use thin sleeping mats which could be hung from a tree. You could slip card between the reeds, or use small bits of wire to provide hooks for any material you wanted to display. This worked well unless it was windy or wet. 9
Teacher trainer, Ghana

It is especially appropriate for use in teaching or training situations where there are no solid walls to display material, in mud houses or classrooms for example. It can be free-standing, mounted on a wall or hung from a ceiling or tree. It can be made of wood, lino, cork, cardboard, woven mats or other materials.

How to make a display board

To make a display board, you first need to decide which materials you are going to use. Then follow the instructions below.

You will need
▶ something to make the surface of the board, for example: cork, cloth (such as felt), lino, wood (plywood, chipboard), cardboard, cement bags or woven mats
▶ something to make the frame, for example, four short lengths of bamboo or strips of wood
▶ a short length of wire to make a hook
▶ nails or tacks
▶ paint (optional)
▶ drawing pins, tacks or sharpened matchsticks for attaching items to the board

What you need to do

1 Make a frame, using lengths of bamboo or wood. Tie or nail them together to form a rectangle.

2 Make a hanging hook from a loop of wire. Attach it to the middle of one of the longer sides of the rectangle.

3 Place the surface material on the frame and fix it using nails or tacks.

4 Paint the surface, if you wish.

Other ways of making a display board

▶ Attach a strip of wood or bamboo to the top and bottom of a piece of cloth, such as a blanket. Add weights along the bottom strip to help it to hang straight. Attach a hook to the reverse of the top strip.

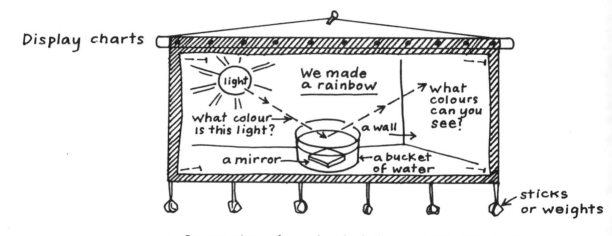

▶ Cover a piece of wood with cloth, or paint it. Attach a hook to the reverse.

▶ Open up a cardboard box to make a zigzag board, or keep it closed to make a cube-shaped display.

▶ Make a beam from a piece of wood or bamboo. Hang it on the wall using nails or loops of wire. Hook pieces of wire over the beam to display items.

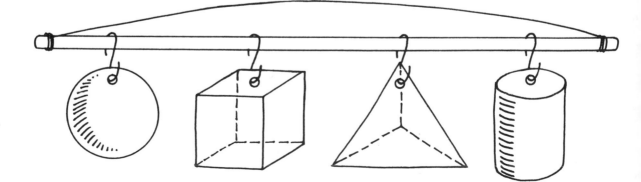

❛ We were keen to have a permanent display of photographs, maps and charts relating to the project... The trouble was that they either went missing or got very dog-eared from people touching them. A local craftsman made some glass-fronted cabinets which he screwed to the walls. They not only solved the problem but added prestige to what was felt by some in the department to be an unimportant part of their work (involving communities and especially women in planning, implementation, operation and maintenance of water and sanitation systems). **❜**
Community worker, Pakistan

How to use a display board

In the classroom, displays can be made of the students' work, such as art and crafts, or maps and charts. This is particularly useful for project work when they have been working in groups: students of different abilities can work together on tasks that are equally important. One student can be responsible for illustrations, while another can understand texts and use that knowledge to contribute to the project's display, possibly using bar charts and so on (see pages 67–73). This type of group participation builds the confidence of less able students and challenges the more able students.

Remember not to leave a display up for too long, or it will stop attracting attention. For transporting a display board, first take off all the pictures and objects. Arrange the display again at your destination.

Magnet boards

Magnet boards are metal boards on which images and figures mounted on magnetic backing can be placed and moved about. They are useful aids to telling stories, demonstrating something or 'acting out' a drama. Magnet boards can be used in similar ways to flannelboards (see pages 33–35). They are ideal for using in the classroom situation and in training sessions.

How to make a magnet board and magnetic symbols

You will need
► purpose-made thin iron sheeting for the magnet board. (You can also use recycled material, such as metal mosquito netting, old metal office shelving, an old metal sign, or flattened out vegetable oil tins.)
► glue
► small magnets for the magnetic symbols
► cards
► magazines

If you cut open tins of vegetable oil and flatten them for sheeting, be careful of the sharp edges.

What you need to do to make the magnetic symbols

1 Draw or paint the symbols/figures you want on card, or cut out images from magazines and stick them on card.

2 Cut the symbols out of the card.

3 Stick the symbols onto small magnets.

Try not to drop the magnets too often, because they will lose their magnetism.

If you paint the magnet board with black non-glare (matt) paint it can be used as a chalkboard too.

One of the advantages of magnet boards is that they are wind-resistant, and so can be used outside on a windy day.

How to use a magnet board

Move the magnetic figures around by picking them up and placing them in different positions on the magnet board. They will remain attached to the board until you want to move them again. This is useful in story-telling, especially when sequences are repeated. More drama can be introduced if the scene is built up as the story is told. The magnet board can also be used with students in small groups – they can use it to re-tell a story.

Memory games can be used in the classroom with the magnet board, for example Kim's game. In this game a number of objects are attached to the board. The students have one minute to look at them. The board is then turned around and the students have a few minutes to write down every object they remember seeing on the board.

In training sessions, learners can make their own magnet boards to take back and use in their own communities.

Flannelboard

A flannelboard (or flannelgraph) is a board covered in felt or other rough fabric, or simply a large piece of rough cloth such as a blanket. Pictures with a rough backing, such as sandpaper, are placed on the board. It is usually hung or slanted at an angle so that the pictures stay on.

Two types of flannelboard can be made:
► using a solid frame, or the back of an existing board
► a soft display – a piece of flannel with a pole at the top and bottom

Flannelboards can be used for displays to impart information both in the classroom and in training sessions. They are effective in teaching individuals as well as groups, particularly people who do not read well or who are non-literate, when they are useful for relaying specific health and nutrition messages.

In some countries it is possible to buy flannelboards cheaply from government departments or NGOs. Otherwise, they are simple to make.

How to make a flannelboard

You will need
► a board or thin piece of plywood
► a piece of dark material, about 1.3 m × 1.3 m
► enough material (preferably felt) to make:
  – about 25 figures, for example, people, animals and houses
  – headings to enable you or the group to enact a familiar situation

You may also need:
► magazine pictures
► stiff card
► coloured wool
► glue
► sandpaper or sand

If you do not have a free-standing board, you could use a mat on the ground. Some teachers and development workers believe this works more effectively. Others use a blanket folded over the back of a chair.

What you need to do to make the flannelboard
1 Cover the board or plywood with the dark cloth (or use the reverse side of a free-standing chalkboard or whiteboard).

2 Use tacks, nails or drawing pins to fix it in position, depending on whether a temporary or permanent flannelboard is required.

3 Angle the board so that it slopes slightly away from you at the top and towards you at the bottom.

What you need to do to make the flannelboard figures

Either:

Cut the shapes out of felt. This is the best material for flannelboard shapes.

Or:

If you do not have any felt, cut shapes from magazines and glue them onto strong card. To make them stick to the board, glue a small piece of sandpaper on the back of each one, or sprinkle some sand on a small glued piece of paper instead.

Remember when making your own figures that scale is important. If a cockroach is bigger than a house, it will confuse your teaching message.

How to use a flannelboard

In the classroom, flannelboards are used for telling stories. As with the magnet board, the teacher places the pictures on the flannelboard while the story is told. Individual students can place the pictures on the flannelboard too, so that the class can be involved in the story. The students' attention is then focused on the visual aid and this helps them to remember the story and the language.

The following are suggestions for a successful lesson or session:
▶ keep all the pictures in clearly marked bags or envelopes
▶ before the lesson, plan where you will place each picture
▶ organise the pictures in the order they will be used
▶ create the scenes as they happen in the story
▶ take the pictures off the board when you have finished using them.

For the final part of the story, have a visual display on the board that the students or audience will remember. Then put the pictures back in the marked bags or envelopes. The flannelboard can remain hanging up or be put into a clearly labelled plastic bag with a mothball.

In some communities, adults may feel uncomfortable about standing up and using a flannelboard. However, if it is laid in the middle of a circle of people sitting on the floor, it can be a more friendly and acceptable training aid in development work.

❝ You can hang a flannelboard anywhere, either by tying it up or securing it with drawing pins or nails. It can be rolled up and carried easily. Sometimes we would do a health message using the flannelboard for the people waiting at outpatients, but most seemed puzzled by the procedure. However, its effect was very different in a training session. It was very good for teaching. ❞
Community health co-ordinator, Bangladesh

Flexi-flan figures

Flexi-flans (sometimes called flexis) are used on flannelboards. They are usually made of paper and have jointed arms, legs and bodies. These can be moved to show a range of actions.

Like flannelboard figures, flexi-flan figures are a communication tool that can be used to demonstrate information or perhaps to enable trainees or a group to share learning or their feelings about themselves, their workplace or their community.

Flexi-flans can be used in a spontaneous way and are excellent if you are teaching or working with a mixed group of literate and non-literate people.

❝ I was training some engineers and local government workers and used flexi-flans to show them the creative possibilities of open-ended communication tools like these. One man took three figures and placed them some distance from each other and looking in different directions. 'This is my department, this is the engineering department and this is your organisation,' he said. 'We are not communicating: that is why nothing gets done.' The following discussion revealed more than I had understood from two months of working with the project. ❞
Water and sanitation communications trainer, Pakistan

How to make flexi-flan figures

Flexi-flan figures are quick and easy to make so you may prefer to have new figures for each training session. If community groups have made the figures themselves, you should leave the figures with them.

The students or learners could make their own flexi-flan figures or you could prepare them in advance.

You will need
▶ magazine pictures
▶ paint
▶ cloth
▶ cardboard or heavyweight paper
▶ scissors
▶ press-studs or brass headed split pins
▶ a hole punch

What you need to do

1 Draw patterns for the body parts of the following figures: adult male, adult female, child male, child female. The adult figures should be 20-40 cm high and the children will be smaller. The body parts you will need to draw are:
  ▶ head – draw a side view so that you can make some figures look to the right and some to the left
  ▶ body – the head and upper body could be one piece, jointed with the lower body at the waist, or the head and body could be separate, jointed at the neck
  ▶ arms – either in one piece or in two pieces jointed at the elbow
  ▶ legs – either in one piece (if they are going to be hidden under a skirt) or in two pieces jointed at the knee (if they are going to have trousers).

When drawing the patterns, remember to extend the length of the parts that join so there is enough overlap to make the joint with the press-stud or split pin.

2 Use the patterns to make as many body parts as you need for the figures you are making. Cut the parts from light cardboard or heavyweight paper.

3 Paint the faces. To make the clothes you can either paint them or glue pieces of fabric in place. You might find it easier to cover the card with paint or fabric before you cut the body part out.

4 Join the parts together to make each figure. Use the hole punch to make holes at the joints for the split pins or press the halves of the press-studs through from the back and the front, and snap them together.

Make some figures face left and some face right, so they can be made to look as if they are having a conversation.

When storing flexi-flan figures, keep them in a dry place, out of direct sunlight. Label the bag or box they are put in.

How to use flexi-flan figures

In some societies, the figures work better if laid on the ground in the middle of a group of people. You will also need to work this way if you do not have a flannelboard.

When working with students, you can use the figures to tell stories. Move the figures about to show what is going on in the story and ask the students questions about who the characters are and what they are doing.

Students can write their own stories or short plays and present them to the class using the figures.

Flipchart

A flipchart is a series of sheets of paper, fastened together at the top. When a sheet has been used, it can be 'flipped' over the top so that the next sheet can be used.

You may purchase ready-made flipcharts, or you can make your own.

Flipcharts may be:
► unmounted, and therefore easy to transport
► mounted on a board, such as a chalkboard
► mounted, but free-standing

How to make an unmounted flipchart

This flipchart will need to be held by the teacher or trainer. If you add the pole it can be hung from a wall or hooked over another board, such as a chalkboard.

You will need
► sheets of paper
► two thin strips of wood the same length as the top edge of your sheets of paper
► nails or screws
► a pole slightly longer than the strips of wood (optional)
► string (optional)
► wire (optional)

What you need to do
1 If you are going to hang the chart from a pole, drill a hole at each end of both strips of wood. Make sure the positions of the holes match.

2 Place one strip of wood underneath the pile of paper, along one of the shorter edges. Place the second strip in the same position on top of the pile of paper. Make sure the holes are in line.

6 In Thailand there were lots of whiteboards, big and small, so we could take whiteboards to villages. I used to draw silhouettes of cattle, but because it was best to prepare these in advance, a flipchart was often more useful. **9**
Beef cattle extension officer, Thailand

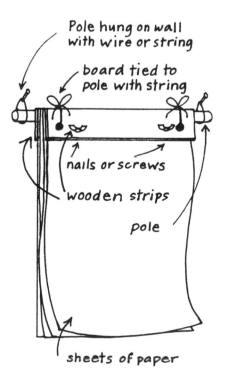

Pole hung on wall with wire or string

board tied to pole with string

nails or screws

wooden strips

pole

sheets of paper

3 Nail or screw the strips of wood together, through the paper, so all the sheets are held tightly together.

4 To hang the chart from the pole, make holes in the sheets of paper through the holes you made earlier in the strips of wood. Thread string through the holes and tie the flip chart to the pole.

5 Either make two hooks from wire and attach them to far ends of the pole, at the back, or make two loops from string. The flipchart can now be hung on the wall and the sheets can be folded back behind the pole.

The chart can be rolled up for easy transport.

How to make a mounted flipchart

The following instructions are for mounting a large flipchart (A3 size or larger) on a sheet of plywood. You could adapt the size of the board if you are going to use smaller sheets of paper but, if you are going to use it with large groups of people, the sheets need to be as large as possible.

You will need
► sheets of paper
► a piece of plywood or similar material, approximately 50 cm × 75 cm
► a long strip of plywood the same length as the top edge of the board and 5 cm wide
► two bolts and two wing nuts

What you need to do
1 Drill two holes at the top of the plywood board approximately 15 cm from each end. Note: this will depend on the size of your paper, so read the instructions and check the size carefully before you start.

2 Drill two matching holes in the wooden strip.

3 Position a sheet of paper slightly below the top of the plywood board and centre it. Make two holes in the paper that correspond to the holes in the board.

4 Using the first sheet as a template, make holes in all the other sheets of paper.

5 Place the bolts through the back of the board and through the holes in all the sheets of paper. Place the wooden strip over the sheets and insert the bolts through the holes.

6 Fasten the wing nuts to hold the paper and wood strip firmly.

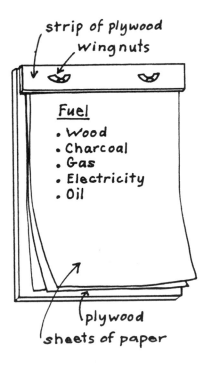

strip of plywood
wingnuts

Fuel
• Wood
• Charcoal
• Gas
• Electricity
• Oil

plywood
sheets of paper

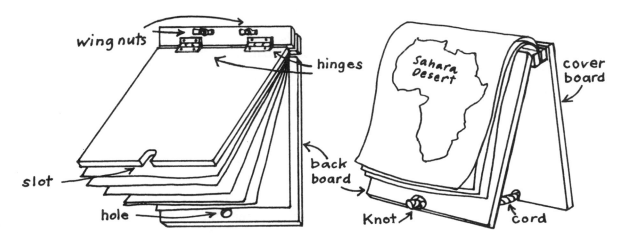

How to make a free-standing, mounted flipchart

These instructions are for a smaller flipchart.

You will need
- ► two pieces of plywood or similar material, approximately 45 cm × 50 cm
- ► two strips of plywood the same length as the top edge of the board and 5 cm wide
- ► two bolts and two wing nuts
- ► four hinges and screws
- ► a piece of cord or string

What you need to do
1 Drill two holes in each wooden strip, approximately 15 cm from each end.

2 Hinge each strip to a piece of plywood.

3 Align the top edge of a sheet of paper with the top edge of a wooden strip. Punch two holes through the paper corresponding to the holes in the strip.

4 Use this sheet as template, and punch holes in all the other sheets you are going to use.

5 Drill a small hole near the bottom edge of one of the sheets of plywood. This is the back board.

6 In the other sheet of plywood, cut a vertical slot about 2 mm wide and 1.5 cm long. This is the cover board.

7 Place your sheets of paper between the two wooden strips and line up the holes.

8 Insert the bolts through the back board, the paper and the cover board, and secure with the wing nuts at the front.

9 To make the flipchart stand up, flip the cover board back to show the first sheet of paper. Pass the cord through the hole in the back board. Make a knot in both ends of the cord to prevent it slipping through the hole. Pull the cord through the slot in the cover board until the second knot catches in it.

& I made different-sized flipcharts depending on the number of people in my audience. In a training session with 15–20 people, I used large plain sheets mounted on an easel where I wrote prepared text and diagrams. The audience then broke into smaller groups and used newsprint flipcharts. Sometimes they tore the sheet off to pin up elsewhere in the room. Out in the field I used smaller, picture flipcharts which were laminated and backed with cardboard so they could stand without other support in front of the group. **9**

Communications consultant, Pakistan

How to use a flipchart

A flipchart can be used in two ways:
- ▶ with blank sheets of paper or newsprint, which the teacher or trainer writes on during the session
- ▶ as a pre-prepared resource with pictures and/or notes. To avoid having to write while speaking, you can prepare texts and drawings before the lesson or session.

Each sheet of a flipchart should illustrate one point or message in a lecture, talk or training session. You should turn to the next sheet when moving on to the next point. This helps students and learners to understand and remember information. It also acts as an aid to you, reminding you of the structure of your lesson or presentation. Development workers find picture flipcharts particularly useful for illustrating important points.

Explanatory or additional notes can be written on the back of the previous page to remind you of what you need to say or to provide information in case you are asked detailed questions. This is particularly helpful if a flipchart is to be mass-produced and used by teachers and trainers who have not been involved in its design.

If you are working with several small groups, you can give each group a blank sheet and a pen. After their discussions, the group can write their conclusions on the sheet. The conclusions of all the groups can then be displayed for everyone to see.

Suggestions and ideas from students or trainees can be written on blank sheets of a flipchart to enable them to see their ideas, for example in a planning workshop for teachers. The sheets can be taken away and used for future reference to draw up detailed plans or as notes for a written report.

Useful tips

- ▶ Flipcharts can also be made using screen-printed cloth pictures, nailed to a piece of dowelling. The pictures can be rolled around the dowelling for storage.

- ▶ Paper and card can be laminated for protection. If a professional laminating service is not available, clear sticky-backed plastic or clear plastic bags can be used to cover the sheets.

- ▶ As some felt-tip markers will soak through paper to the next sheet, you may need to prepare each sheet separately before attaching them to the flipchart.

- ▶ Make sure your writing can be seen by the class or audience, and that it is consistent (see Lettering, Chapter 6, pages 109–111).

- ▶ Each character you draw should be consistent. They should look the same in each picture and wear the same clothes.

- ▶ When making a picture flipchart, make sure the pictures are inserted in the correct order.

▶ Picture sheets can be interleaved with blank sheets so that you can write notes during the lesson or session.

Rope and pole display board

A rope and pole display board consists of two parallel, horizontal poles tied loosely together with rope. Visual aids such as posters can be pinned to the rope. This kind of display board is invaluable where there are few solid walls for displaying information. It has no solid backing and can be made quickly for teaching, training and when working with communities.

How to make a rope and pole display board

You will need
▶ two pieces of thin wood, rattan or bamboo (the size will depend on the size of the display required)
▶ string or rope

What you need to do

1 Ask someone to hold the pieces of wood parallel and at least 30 cm apart.

2 Wind the string or rope back and forth between both pieces of wood.

3 Tie another length of string to both ends of one of the pieces of wood to hang it up.

An even quicker version can be made by attaching a length of bamboo along a wall and hanging visual aids on it. Collages, project work and other work can be displayed on these.

There are other different types of rope and pole display board. You can experiment with local materials to discover which works best. In the Indian sub-continent a traditional rope bed, known as a charpoi, can be turned on its side to make an excellent board. A hammock could also be used.

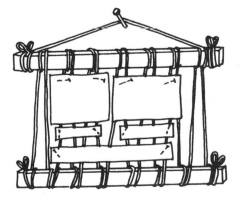
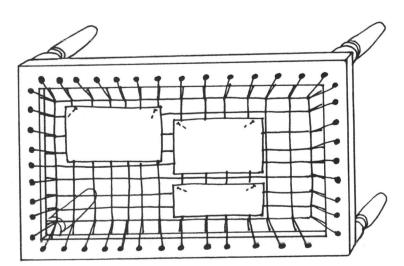

How to use a rope and pole display board

Use pins, staples or glue to attach information to the rope and pole display board. Alternatively, before the board is hung up, slip cards between the string.

Washing-line display

A washing-line display (or string display) looks exactly like a washing-line – a string tied between two poles or trees. It can be used to display or organise information during teaching or training sessions, and is particularly useful for explaining the order of a process. For example, a washing-line display could show how to grow trees:

1 Fence off nursery tree area from chickens, livestock and children.

2 Prepare seed beds.

3 Plant trees in nursery.

4 Transplant young saplings to designated sites.

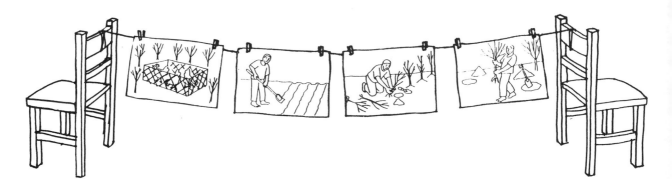

How to make a washing-line display

You will need
► string, clothes line or rope
► clothes pegs, or paperclips if the rope is thin

What you need to do
1 Find somewhere to fix the string or rope to at both ends. You could perhaps use the back of two chairs in a school, but this may be too low for older students or adult learners to see comfortably. Outside, you could tie it between two trees.

2 Use pegs or paperclips to attach the display items to the line.

A washing-line display is best used indoors. If you want to make one outside, make sure it is not a windy day!

If you want to keep the pictures, make sure they are clearly labelled and that the pegs do not damage them.

How to use a washing-line display

When using the washing-line display, you can ask students to decide on the order of a process and the students can pin the visual aids up themselves.

❛ During workshops with cadet journalists I used string display lines to peg up examples of different news stories. The trainees then had to decide which story was the "lead" news story and grade the others in descending order. By dividing the group into two teams I was able to encourage editorial co-operation and develop the ability to recognise the best news story. During these sessions I always stressed that there was no right or wrong answer, but the students were quick to debate the priority given to an item which they thought didn't deserve space on the front page of the newspaper. ❜
Journalist trainer, Papua New Guinea

3

Visual aids which display information

The visual aids in this chapter convey information much more effectively if time is spent planning their design. Tips on good design are given with the instructions for making each one; it is also worth referring to the basic design techniques described in Chapter 6.

If you need help in deciding which visual aid to make, refer to Chapter 1. In this chapter, visual aids which are the most commonly used and simplest to make are described first. You may find it useful to try out basic design techniques on posters and worksheets first, and then progress to pamphlets and newsletters as your skill increases. Photo stories are easily the most ambitious and time-consuming visual aid in this group, but they are extremely popular.

All the visual aids in this chapter can be used with small or large groups in a variety of teaching and training situations. Most can be used indoors or outdoors. Overhead transparencies are the exception, in that they can only be used in a darkened room; you will also need special acetates to make them, a good electricity supply, and an overhead projector. Most of the visual aids in this chapter are made of paper or cloth, and so are easy to transport because they can be folded or rolled up. Posters and wallcharts can be used in schools for project work in science, geography, maths and so on. Flashcards are extremely useful in language and reading lessons in primary classes. The students can also play matching games with the flashcards which helps them to remember the words.

All the visual aids described in this chapter should last well, especially if they are stored carefully; those made of paper or card can be covered with clear plastic where appropriate. This is particularly important for flashcards, because they will be handled a great deal.

Poster

A poster consists of pictures, words and/or numbers drawn on a large, flat sheet of paper, cloth or card. It should be as big as possible with clear illustrations and a short message.

Posters are useful to communicate simple, clear information to individuals and groups (for example, health information) and can be used effectively in both schools and in development work. Before making a poster, you need to think carefully about it and pre-test your initial designs (see Chapter 1, page 14 on pre-testing).

Choosing which language to convey your message can be difficult and sometimes controversial, particularly in development work. Often posters are printed in the language of government, or in

6 We wanted to translate an English language health message into the local language so we asked for help. There were six pre-testers and six different views about how this simple slogan should be translated into Kwangali. It made us realise how important it was to communicate ideas as much as possible. 9
Graphic designer, Namibia

English, as well as the local language. Which is best for your situation?

Language choice is very important, so you should consider the options carefully with your colleagues, local professionals and the pre-test comments from your trial group.

❝ We were sent a series of nice posters to promote a national literacy campaign. But the designs weren't always clear. For example, why was the woman carrying a baby on her back? Why was the child having an injection? If you couldn't read or write, the posters had no clear message. Worse, all of them were printed in English. One slogan said, 'Never too late to learn' above a picture of a teacher with a classroom of adults. The problem was that to help people become literate you need materials in the appropriate language, preferably the local one. ❞
Community radio trainer, Ghana

How to make a poster

You will need
▶ A3 size paper or larger (two sheets of A4 can be taped together) – you could use newsprint or brown paper from the butchers
▶ felt pens or crayons, biros

What you need to do
1 Think carefully about the information you want to include on the poster. Ask yourself 'What is the purpose of the poster?'

2 Practise drawing the picture until you are happy with it. You could involve students, learners or a local artist in this.

3 Practise writing the message until you are happy with it. Decide which language will be the most effective. If the poster is going to be mass-produced, you may need to do several versions of the poster in different languages.

4 When you are happy with your picture and the wording, pre-test it before you produce the finished poster. Make any changes that may be necessary.

5 Produce the final version of the poster.

Remember that the most effective posters have clear, uncomplicated pictures and short written messages. The clearest and cheapest posters use simple black and white drawings.

Read the relevant sections of Chapter 6 about basic techniques:
Colour, page 102
Drawing, pages 104–107
Lettering, pages 109–111.

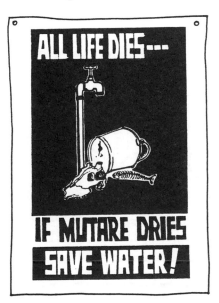

This poster was produced in Mutare, Zimbabwe during the 1992 drought

How to use posters

Posters are very useful in students' project work. Divide the class into groups and each group can decide what message their poster is going to have. The completed posters, together with the students' other project work, such as reports and maps, can then be displayed around the school.

❝ We had very little time to produce posters for a Health Campaign parade, so one of my colleagues did some large, neat lettering on an A4 piece of paper saying 'Keep healthy – eat more fish.' This was then enlarged on the photocopier. It wasn't original, but the message was clear, it was quick to produce and the 25 we made caught people's attention during the parade through town. ❞
Fisheries Officer, South Pacific

Wallchart

A wallchart is a large flat printed sheet of paper, card or cloth, which records and displays related sets of information. A wallchart contains much more information than a poster, which usually conveys only one message. A wallchart can be used as a teaching chart for a lesson: it must then be large enough for the whole class to see.

A wallchart can also be made and used in development work to record and display information.

Wallcharts are used for monitoring progress in a community forestry project over (a) one month and (b) six months

COMMUNITY FORESTRY MONITORING CHART — MONTH June

Rating			NURSERY	TREE PLANTING	FERTILIZER	EXTENSION SUPPORT	GROUP MEETING	LOAN REPAYMENTS	FUELWOOD	FODDER	FRUITS	SOIL IMPROVEMENT	VISITORS
😀	5	😊			✓	✓	✓						
🙂	4	🙂	✓										✓
😐	3	😕							✓	✓		✓	
😠	2	🙁									✓		
😫	1	😣		✓				✓					

COMMUNITY FORESTRY MONITORING CHART

Rating		Month	NURSERY	TREE PLANTING	FERTILIZER	EXTENSION SUPPORT	GROUP MEETING	LOAN REPAYMENTS	FUELWOOD	FODDER	FRUITS	SOIL IMPROVEMENT	VISITORS
😀	5	January	3	3	4	5	4	2	2	3	4	3	1
🙂	4	February	3	4	4	4	4	3	3	3	4	4	2
😐	3	March	4	4	3	5	5	3	3	4	4	3	3
😠	2	April											
		May											
😫	1	June											

Wallcharts are useful as they can illustrate information without the need for explanation from a professional. They should be displayed where a number of people have access to them, for example, in a school, clinic or community building. For transportation purposes you can roll wallcharts up.

How to make a wallchart

You will need
- ▶ A3 sized paper or larger (for more information on paper see Paper, Chapter 6 page 113), a large piece of card, or light-coloured cloth
- ▶ coloured crayons, marker pens
- ▶ information for the chart, such as diagrams, text, pictures cut from magazines, etc.
- ▶ glue
- ▶ scissors
- ▶ a large piece of sticky-backed plastic

What you need to do
1 Decide what information is required on the wallchart.

2 Sketch it first and then pre-test it. Make any changes that may be necessary.

3 Draw, paint or glue the final pictures, diagrams and text onto the large piece of card or paper. Pre-test it again.

4 Cover the final version with sticky-backed plastic for durability.

Banner

A banner is a long piece of cloth with words, pictures and/or symbols painted on it or attached to it. Banners are excellent for attracting the attention of a large group of people. They can be used either indoors or outside, carried on poles or hung from walls, trees or buildings. They are particularly good to use at special events, such as school sports days and opening ceremonies.

❝ Our team was working to improve child nutrition. We made a huge picture of a healthy baby and then surrounded it with pictures from the four food groups that should be eaten each day to make up a nutritious diet. Occasionally one of the women had problems understanding the wallchart, but because it was in the village hall, where people could refer to it whenever they wanted, someone always seemed to be willing to explain its message. ❞
Nurse, Sierra Leone

6 If you plan to march with the banner, it is advisable to make some holes in the banner, or to make large banners in two strips, joined together by a short strip of bamboo. This prevents the banner from puffing out and the banner-holders from having to battle against the wind. **9**

Graphic artist, Namibia

How to make a banner

You will need
- ▶ plain cotton material (or flour or rice sacks)
- ▶ brightly coloured material or paints
- ▶ bamboo, thin pieces of wood or a rod (for handles and stiffeners)
- ▶ tassels and long thin strips of cloth for streamers
- ▶ needle and thread
- ▶ glue

What you need to do

1 Decide with the student group:
- ▶ which words and pictures are to be shown on the banner
- ▶ how it is to be hung and used.

2 Draw the design on a sheet of paper the same size as the banner. Divide the paper into sections so it is easy to space the letters and words.

You may prefer to use a letter stencil.

3 When you are happy with the design, transfer it to the cotton material. Pencil the lines in. You could divide the banner into sections, as you did on the paper, if it helps.

4 When everything is placed correctly on the material, you can start painting, sewing or gluing the letters.

5 Add tassels and streamers to the edges of the banner.

6 If the banner is long, stop it sagging in the middle by sewing a horizontal pocket along the top and inserting a long, thin rod or piece of bamboo.

Refer to the relevant sections of Chapter 6 for basic techniques:
Colour, page 102
Glue, pages 108–109
Lettering, pages 109–111
Paint, page 112.

Clothing poster

A clothing poster is a small poster with a message or picture on it, which is pinned or taped to the clothes someone is wearing. Clothing posters can stimulate discussion, and increase vocabulary and literacy skills, and are a useful teaching tool with all age groups.

Clothing posters are usually used as a game to develop students' language skills; students can learn words that are opposites or are related to each other. For adults, this game can be a good 'ice breaker' exercise (for getting to know one another) at the beginning of a training session.

6 At an adult literacy class, students had to pair up with the person who had a connected word on their clothing poster. For example, one woman discovered that she had the word 'sand' and then had to find the person with 'beach'. Other pairs were 'chair/table', 'coffee/cup' and 'sun/moon'. **9**

Adult literacy teacher, Maldives

How to use clothing posters

The objective of this game is for participants with matching or corresponding posters to pair up:

1 They have to discover what or who is on the poster on their back by asking questions like: Is the word/picture an animal? Is it an object? Is it big or small?, until they have guessed the right answer.

2 Then they have to find their partner. For example, if they discover that their word is 'water', they must pair up with something connected to water, such as 'river' or 'sea'.

With primary school students or non-literate participants, you could draw a simple line drawing or use a picture cut from a magazine.

How to make a clothing poster

You will need
► A5 size pieces of paper (paper bags could be used)
► marker pens
► safety pins or tape to secure the posters to clothes

What you need to do

1 Write your words or messages, or draw your pictures, on the pieces of paper. Make sure that you do not offend people with the characters, animals, colours or objects that you select for the posters.

2 Pre-test them to be sure that participants will recognise which words or pictures are paired or related.

3 Attach the posters to the backs of the participants' clothes. Do not let them see what their word or picture is. Take care not to tear anyone's clothes.

Wall painting

A wall painting (a mural) can be a highly effective visual aid. It can be used to convey health, nutrition and literacy messages, as well as local information. Ends of buildings in busy public places, such as schools and hospital wards, are ideal.

It is essential to pre-test your design for a mural. Because murals are very public and long-lasting, ideally the whole school/community should decide the content of the mural.

How to make a wall painting

You will need
► paint or coloured chalks
► charcoal

A grid enlarging system may also be helpful (see Enlargements, pages 107–108).

What you need to do

1 Make sure that you have permission to use the wall.

2 Decide what message the mural is going to convey.

3 Sketch out your design and pre-test it to check that it is appropriate and effective. Make any changes that may be necessary.

4 Check that the surface of the wall will 'take' the paint. Test different types of paint on a small area. The colour and texture of the wall may change the colour of your paint. It may also absorb the paint very quickly, which means that you will have to use larger amounts of paint.

5 If possible, wash the wall and allow it to dry.

6 Mark the outline of your design on the wall using chalk, charcoal or a thin line of paint.

7 Paint the mural.

Refer to the relevant sections of Chapter 6 for basic techniques:
Chalk, page 101
Colour, page 102
Design, page 103
Drawing, pages 104–107
Enlargements, pages 107–108
Paint, page 112

Worksheet

A worksheet lists questions or activities for students or trainees to work through. Pre-prepared worksheets can be used successfully with groups with differing abilities or language skills because each person can work at their own pace.

How to use worksheets

Worksheets can be used for homework or a revision programme, or they can include further details to be studied for the next lesson.

They can be photocopied, or copies can be made using a jelly copier or banda machine (see Copying, Chapter 6, page 102).

In development work, worksheets can reinforce or remind trainees about a particular message or technique.

Worksheets provide flexibility in the classroom as well as in the workshop, because they can be used individually, in pairs, or in small groups to facilitate teamwork skills.

How to make a worksheet

You will need
▶ paper or card
▶ copying facilities
▶ a typewriter or clear handwriting

What you need to do
1 Think about the aim of the worksheet. For example, it might be to practise a skill, such as subtraction. Make sure the worksheet relates to the lesson plan and the syllabus.

2 Make a draft copy first, to check that you have included everything.

Write clear instructions at the top of the sheet. Leave space for students to write their names at the top of the sheet.

If necessary, leave enough space for students to write their answers or observations on the sheet.

❝ I used a lot of cartoons on my worksheets. The students seemed to prefer a bit of text and then pictures dotted around the worksheet to make it look attractive. It was important that the writing was clear – words tended to smudge on the banda (copier) unless you spaced them out and printed letters rather than doing joined up letters. ❞
English teacher, Zanzibar

3 Produce the final version. Write clearly or type it. Draw any diagrams or pictures clearly.

As worksheets are not durable, keep the master copy (or carbon) in a safe, dry place.

Our School _____   Name . . . .

Fill in the answers to the questions below.

1. How many classes are there? . . . .

2. What is the name of the head teacher? . . . .

3. What colour is the school uniform? . . . .

4. What is the school motto? . . . .
   . . . .

5. Draw the school badge in the space below

Flashcards used to teach reading

Flashcard

Flashcards are small cards with a picture or symbol on them used both in teaching and in development work. In the classroom, flashcards are commonly used to teach reading. A picture, for example, of an elephant may be drawn or stuck on a card and the word 'elephant' written underneath it or on a different card. The students are encouraged to associate the pictures and the words through various 'look and say' activities and games, for example, Kim's game (see page 32), Pairs (see page 89), and so on.

In teaching and development work, flashcards may have pictures or symbols drawn or painted on them. They are particularly useful for stimulating discussion in small groups, as well as for sharing information and reminding people of a recommended process. As with posters, research the local situation and pre-test them.

How to make flashcards

Flashcards can be various sizes depending on their use. For small groups, they can be pocket-sized. For large groups, A4 is best.

You will need
- ▶ strong card
- ▶ marker pens
- ▶ scissors
- ▶ glue
- ▶ pictures (drawn or from magazines)

Flashcards being used to stimulate discussion of health issues

What you need to do

Use simple line drawings, or cut pictures from magazines and glue them onto card. Write the words clearly on the cards (see Lettering, Chapter 6, pages 109–111).

For durability and protection, flashcards can be covered with clear plastic or sticky-backed plastic. Keep them in clearly labelled envelopes, plastic bags or boxes.

How to use flashcards

To use flashcards in a classroom situation, such as learning to read, show the picture and the word together. Ask students to look at the picture and say the word. Then they look at the word and say it again. After presenting a number of words with pictures that the students already know, ask for volunteers to come out and match pictures and words. When the students have learnt to read the words, you can divide them into teams and play reading games using the flashcards.

Overhead transparency

Overhead transparencies (OHTs) are see-through sheets of plastic, usually A4 size, which have words and/or images written, typed or drawn on them. OHTs are also called acetates. An overhead projector (OHP) is an electric light box which is used to project the words on the OHTs onto a screen or a white wall. An overhead projector is an extremely flexible teaching aid which is simple to use and which is available in many countries.

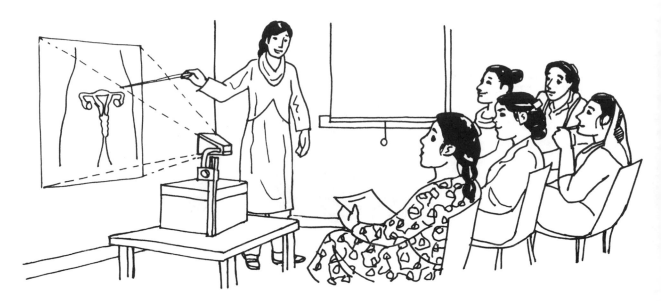

How to make overhead transparencies

You will need
- ▶ acetate sheets, available from stationery shops
- ▶ special soluble pens (washable pens – you can wash the writing off) in different colours, or permanent pens

What you need to do

1 Write a draft before you write on the acetate. It is important not to include too much information. Six or seven points per sheet should be the maximum.

2 Write clearly on the acetate. The letters should be at least 1 cm high. (See Lettering, Chapter 6, pages 109–111.)

It is also possible to photocopy typed or computer-generated sheets onto special acetates. (It is important to use the right type of acetate, or the photocopier could be ruined.) Images from books and magazines can be traced onto acetates too.

Remember to hold OHTs at their edges to avoid fingerprints and scratch marks. Store them in separate, clearly labelled folders with plain paper between each one. They can also be kept in transparent pockets with lecture notes in a ringbinder file.

How to use overhead transparencies

To use OHTs you will need an overhead projector, an electricity supply, something to use as a screen and a way of making the room dark.

To ensure that you are confident with overhead transparencies, practise using them before giving your lectures or training sessions.

- ▶ Set up the overhead projector before the students or trainees arrive. Check that the image is in focus.

❝ The main problem with OHTs is that eight times out of ten there is too much writing on them, so people do not read what is on them. ❞
Photojournalist, Zimbabwe

▶ Darken the room while using the projector so that the images are clearer.

▶ Place the OHTs on the projector the right way up.

▶ To keep the students' or trainees' attention when you are introducing a topic which is not on the acetate, either turn the projector off or cover the acetate with a piece of plain paper.

▶ To highlight particular information while you are speaking, use a pointer such as a thin stick or a car aerial.

You can also use an overhead projector in the same way that you would use a chalkboard. You can write key points on an acetate on the projector while you are speaking, to draw attention to them. You can also overlay several acetates on the projector to build up information. They can be taped down one edge to keep them together.

During workshops small groups can list the main points of their discussions on acetates to present to the whole group at the end of the session.

CASE STUDY Overhead transparencies

During a trainers' workshop for community foresters in Malaysia, the facilitator wanted to show information about nutrient recycling. To go outside and experiment would have taken too long and perhaps been too complicated. Instead she organised a single session in a room with a power supply, an overhead projector and blinds.

The facilitator was not familiar with the centre's projector. So fifteen minutes before the session began she checked that she knew how to turn the projector on and that her acetates and planned overlays were in order.

As the information was quite complex, the facilitator tried to build the picture up in stages. As she says:

'People understand things better when they see information displayed pictorially. If something is quite complex, try to build up a whole picture a stage at a time. Using overlays, I was able to explain about nutrient cycling and the loss of nutrients from soils after logging. For example, my base picture was of a tree and its roots in the soil. Then I put an overlay on top which had arrows showing the nutrient cycle. Finally, I added another

overlay which showed how nutrients are lost if you cut the tree down. There's no doubt that using the projector helped keep my students' attention. The overlay technique also helped because it makes the projected picture more interesting to look at.'

When she had shown all the acetates, the facilitator turned the projector off and asked a participant to put the blinds up to ensure the room cooled down. A question and answer session about the topic helped to ensure participants had understood the information.

Pamphlet

A pamphlet (also called leaflet) consists of handwritten or printed material about a specific topic.

A pamphlet must be clearly and simply written so that people can understand it easily. It is essential, therefore, to research your intended readership. Take time to plan and design your pamphlet carefully. The more pictures it has, and the slimmer it is, the more effective it is likely to be.

How to make a pamphlet

You will need
- ▶ paper
- ▶ a draft of the text you want to use
- ▶ the illustrations you want to use: photographs, line drawings or cartoons
- ▶ pens, or a typewriter
- ▶ glue

What you need to do

1 Decide how many pages you need. A sheet of A4 can make a pamphlet in two ways:
  - ▶ by making one fold down the middle to make a four-page pamphlet (two of these can be stapled together to make an eight-page pamphlet, and so on)
  - ▶ by making two folds to produce a six-page pamphlet (see the illustration below)

How to fold a sheet of A4 to produce a 6-page pamphlet

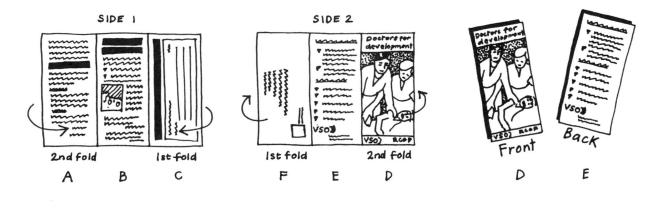

2 Plan what will go on each page. Remember that people notice the front and back most, so these two pages should contain the most important information, and be eye-catching. Make sure there are plenty of illustrations and not too much continuous text.

3 Design each page carefully, and produce a draft for pre-testing.

4 Type or handwrite the final version of the text to fit the spaces you have allowed for it. Read it carefully, and correct any mistakes.

5 Position the text on the pages with the illustrations. Check it carefully again. The pamphlet is ready to be printed or photocopied.

When the pamphlets have been printed, store them in a dry place away from direct sunlight.

Read the relevant sections of Chapter 6 for basic techniques:
Copying, page 102
Drawing, pages 104–107
Lettering, pages 109–111.

Pamphlets are easier to produce if you know how to use and have access to a computer and a desk-top publishing (DTP) programme.

Newsletter

A newsletter is an informal printed report which is distributed to members of a particular group in order to share information. They can be any size, although they are often one sheet of A4 printed on both sides.

A newsletter can be useful to promote good public relations, offering evidence that the school, college or other organisation is working hard to achieve its targets.

To keep a record of newsletters you have made, punch holes in them and store them in a special file.

Printing costs can be funded through selling advertising space or asking local businesses to sponsor a page. Careful budget control is necessary.

Like pamphlets, newsletters are easier to produce if you know how to use and have access to a computer and a desk-top publishing (DTP) programme.

How to make a newsletter

You will need
▶ paper
▶ glue
▶ draft text, including contributions from others and possibly advertisements
▶ illustrations, line drawings and photographs
▶ a typewriter, or computing equipment
▶ copying or printing facilities
▶ a budget

What you need to do
1 Decide on what is going into the newsletter well in advance of the planned distribution date. The needs of the intended readers and the resources available have to be taken into account.

2 Contact local printers and/or photocopy suppliers to get prices for the work. Remember that a quote (quotation) is a fixed price, but an estimate is not. They can also give advice on the cost of different options, for example line drawings may be cheaper to print than photographs.

3 Draw up a schedule with deadlines for copy (articles, features, letters, advertisements), artwork (pictures, photographs, cartoons), proofs (draft copies) and the final version. If other members of the group have been asked to submit copy, or outside experts have been commissioned, they should be given ample time. Let everyone concerned know what the schedule dates are.

4 Decide on an appropriate and attractive layout with colleagues, students or trainees.

5 Write clear headlines and make the captions large enough to be easily read. Use pictures that tell a story and try to keep all text brief.

When writing news items or features answer the questions: Who? What? Where? When? Why? How?

Keep feature items to one page.

List the contents near the front.

If you are producing a long newsletter which is going to be printed, always make the number of pages divisible by four.

6 When all the elements are ready, physically arrange the separate items on the pages. When everyone is satisfied with the page, paste it up, that is, glue the items onto the paper.

7 The pasted version can be either photocopied or typeset and printed.

Plan for a 4-page newsletter

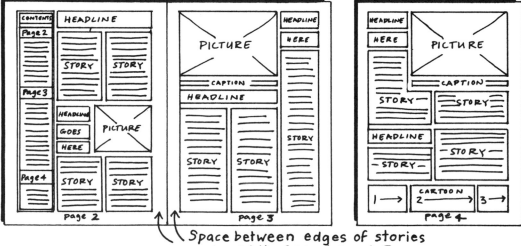

Space between edges of stories and middle fold at least 3 cm

Cartoon

A cartoon is a simple picture of an amusing situation; sometimes it is a satirical comment on a serious or topical issue. A strip cartoon is a sequence of framed drawings which tell a story. Both types are to be found in newspapers, magazines and leaflets.

In development situations a cartoon is a method of conveying a specific message. What is important is that:
▶ the message or story must be simple
▶ people realise that the story must be read in a certain sequence to understand it.

How to make a cartoon

You will need
▶ scrap paper
▶ good quality paper
▶ pencils and/or a fine-nibbed ink or graphic design pen (for example, Rotring)

What you need to do
1 Think carefully about the message you are going to convey. Many of the most effective cartoons are simple pictures which convey meaning at a glance.

2 Try different ways of illustrating your message on scraps of paper until you have isolated the main ideas.

3 Pre-test your ideas with your colleagues and a sample of the intended readers.

4 Draw the final version on good quality paper.

Refer to the relevant sections of Chapter 6 for basic techniques:
Drawing, pages 104–107
Lettering, pages 109–111.

Useful tips

▶ When designing a strip cartoon, it is helpful to number each picture to show readers which picture to look at next. If your audience is unlikely to recognise numbers, you will need to use arrows or another convention to show in which order the pictures should be looked at. Pre-testing can help you to find out which symbol will be the most easily understood. Remember also that many languages are read from right to left, so this will then be the natural way to look at a cartoon strip.

▶ If your readers are not accustomed to seeing cartoons, they may not understand the speech bubble convention. In Nepal pre-testing revealed that many people thought that the speech bubble was garlic, because of its shape. In such a situation, you could write the words as a caption underneath the cartoon.

❝ The first time I made a cartoon picture was to fill a small space in the magazine we were working on. It had four panels and I noticed that people did not know how to read it. They looked at the last picture and laughed, and then looked at the picture beside it – so it was impossible for them to understand the story. ❞
Graphic designer, Solomon Islands

▶ In some countries, cartoons may be a locally-used form of communication. If so, your cartoons will be more effective if you become familiar with the local style and use it.

❝ We were producing a booklet and decided to explain some complicated ecological problems by using simple cartoons. The problem was that sea turtles' eggs in the hatchery must not be turned because this spoils the development of the embryo. We illustrated this by three cartoon drawings of the inside of an egg. In the first you could see a turtle sleeping comfortably in a hammock (the type the conservation park workers used during patrols). The next had a person twisting the egg which made the turtle fall out of the hammock. And the third cartoon was of the turtle having his head bandaged. It was simple, but the message seemed to be clear to everyone. ❞

Conservation adviser, Thailand

A cartoon produced by a teaching aid developer in Pakistan

How to use cartoons

Cartoon pictures can enable people to discuss sensitive issues and so are useful for teaching and training.

Listening skills in the language class can be extended and developed using cartoon strips. You can read out a description of something which needs to be drawn in sequence, each part in a separate frame. Ask the students to listen carefully, while you read the piece two or three times. Then ask them to draw what they have heard. You could provide a template with a number of ready-drawn frames for them to fill in. You could do this with two separate groups and ask the students to discuss what they see in the picture. You can then evaluate how well they have understood the piece you read.

Cartoon strips can be used to teach sequencing and ordering to students. Find, or draw, a cartoon strip with between three and eight separate frames. Cut out each frame and rearrange them so that they are in the wrong order. Stick them down in the new order and make one copy for each group. Ask them to cut each frame out and put them in the correct order. Before you do this, show the students an example on the chalkboard of pictures in the wrong order and ask them to put them in the correct sequence.

The above exercise can also be used in a workshop or training session, using a topic related to the subject of the workshop or session. As it encourages discussion and team decision-making, it can be introduced as an ice-breaker. The less obvious the order, the more interactive the process will be as each group may suggest different answers. This creates an opportunity for each group to explain their answers and defend their position.

If the cartoon is to be used as a discussion starter with a group, *either*
- ▶ make one large cartoon (using enlargement techniques – see Chapter 6, pages 107–108) and protect it with plastic

or
- ▶ make a small one and copy it for distribution using either a photocopier or a jelly copier (see Chapter 6, pages 102–103).

Comic story books

A comic story book is a useful visual aid for communicating a complicated topic (for example, why you need to protect your sea resources) in the classroom or a training session. It might have six frames (a frame is a small cartoon picture which tells a part of the comic story), or it could have more than a hundred.

The best comic story books have a clear beginning, middle and end, and are relevant to the local situation. As with cartoons, it is important to think carefully about what message you wish to convey and the length of the story. Then develop a story which makes the message clear for the people who will read it. Pre-test it with local people.

You could practise creating a comic story book by translating a well-known story into cartoon form. Decide which are the important parts of the story and fit them into a limited number of squares.

Readers who lack confidence and those who are not literate often prefer to look at comics.

6 I was asked to make a comic about population growth for a development education NGO. With my counterparts we developed the story of 'Elsie and Jake' who had hundreds of children. Their storyline borrowed the traditional local belief that babies were found under stones. Despite the delicate subject matter, the comic was non-controversial, so it had a wide readership. The comic worked well because it made people laugh as they recognised their own problems and those that very large families experience. 9
Graphic artist, Solomon Islands

How to make a comic story book

You will need
- ▶ scrap paper to sketch your ideas
- ▶ good quality paper to draw the final cartoons
- ▶ A3 size paper: some scrap for designing the book, and some good quality for the final version
- ▶ pencils and a fine-nibbed ink or graphic design pen (for example, Rotring)
- ▶ photocopying facilities

What you need to do

1 Decide on the story, or stories, you want to include in the book.

2 Plan the stories roughly on some A3 size scrap paper. Fold it in half to form a book. You will need to be sure that the stories fit on the pages. Decide how long the book will be – four pages, eight pages, or more?

Remember that you will need to leave space for the titles of the stories.

3 Sketch your stories in their frames and position them on the rough pages. Follow the instructions for making cartoons on page 59.

4 Pre-test the book, and make any changes necessary.

5 Produce the final drawings in ink and position them on the good quality paper with the lettering for the titles. Remember to number the pages.

6 Photocopy the book for distribution.

Refer to the relevant sections of Chapter 6 for basic techniques:
Drawing, pages 104–107
Lettering, pages 109–111.

You do not need great artistic ability to draw cartoons. However, if you want to make a comic story book then you or a colleague need to be able to draw simple, amusing pictures.

Photo story

As in a comic book, a photo story tells a story using a sequence of pictures in frames, but in this case the pictures are photographs. Speech is indicated by words in speech bubbles coming from the characters' mouths, or with captions and linking sentences between frames. Photo stories are particularly useful for teaching and training because they use realistic images and scenes to present difficult or culturally sensitive information. They have emotional appeal because facial expressions and, therefore, personal feelings can be conveyed. They have been very successful in South America and for AIDS awareness in South Africa.

Photo stories are quite complex to make, you will need some experience of taking photographs to do it successfully. You will also need to budget carefully as photo stories can be expensive to produce.

How to make a photo story

You will need
- a camera
- a flash
- different lenses
- a tripod
- film – black and white film is better than colour if you intend to photocopy the photo story, and it is also cheaper if you intend to print the story
- a large piece of paper – to draw the storyboard
- office equipment – stapler, and so on
- typewriter/word processor – to type out captions
- suitable props (chairs, tables, food, and so on)
- appropriate locations (house, school, park, marketplace)
- actors and actresses (or students/people prepared to enact scenes)
- a planned budget for:
  - printing or photocopying costs
  - film processing
  - distribution

What you need to do
1 Decide what the message or topic of the photo story will be. You can involve your students or group in choosing a topic which is important to them and in planning how the story should be told.

Your project may need to provide information about caring for health or the environment. You may want to raise issues and be thought-provoking about social and political subjects, such as domestic violence, teenage pregnancy or land rights. Choose a short title for the photo story which reflects that message, for example, 'The killer disease'.

2 Make a storyboard. This is a plan of each page of the photo story which tells the actors and photographer what each photo will show. Underneath write the caption or the words the character will speak.

If you can, buy a few copies of commercially-produced photo-comics to give you ideas. Spend as much time as possible thinking about and revising the storyboard to make sure your photo story tells a story, and has a beginning, a middle and an end.

To make the storyboard:
a Draw a series of square boxes in the order you expect the final photo story to be (for example, six to nine frames to a page of A4).
b Write a description of the scene, if you find it too difficult to draw.
c Decide what text is required including speech, explanations and linking sentences. See 3 below.

A storyboard conveys what you want to achieve so it is essential to make one, particularly if someone else is taking the photographs. Check that each picture makes a definite point and that the whole photo story is not too long.

3 Decide how many pictures will need to be taken to advance the story, and what each should show. The number you choose will depend on how many pictures you can fit onto an A5 or A4 page (not more than nine). Remember to put in some close-up shots of the characters when they are just thinking – their thoughts can be written in a 'bubble'. This will make the photo story look more varied and interesting than just using distance shots.

4 Decide what text will be required. Some text will be speech bubbles to show what individual characters think or say. Remember that the words should reflect the character: if, for example, your character is a teenager from a city, or a grandmother from a rural village, choose words which such a person would really use. Otherwise readers will not believe your story.

Other text, such as a short sentence which explains what is happening or which helps link the story to the next photograph, will be shown at the bottom of each picture.

5 Pre-test the story board before the photographs are taken.

6 Now arrange the 'shoot'. This is the session during which the photographs are taken. It may be necessary to have two or more shoots, especially if day and night scenes and different locations are included.

Development workers will need to find people to act out the scenes: friends, members of the local community. Teachers can

❝ Even if you have asked a professional or good amateur photographer to help, you should still check each image is the way you want it, by looking through the viewfinder before the photos are taken. This way you can save time and expense by minimising wasted shots. ❞
Journalist, Mexico

ask for students to volunteer. The story will need to be explained to them.

You will also need to take decisions about hair styles, make-up and so on. There has to be a 'director', (yourself, a student or a trainee) who organises the way the people stand, sit or lie, including their facial expressions for each scene.

You will also need to collect the props, such as tables, chairs, and so on.

Once you have 'actors', the location for the shoot and the props, you can start to take the photographs. The tips over the page will help you to avoid problems when taking photographs.

7 Arranging the photo story. When the photos have been developed you need to select those you will use and arrange them in chronological story order, preferably numbering each photo. Then add the relevant text. If you have a very limited budget, photocopy the photo story (it will reproduce much better if you used black and white film) or talk to a printing company about printing it. In general small quantities are more expensive to print per copy than large numbers.

When making the photo story you will need to remind people how to hold photos – with clean hands at the edge – and discourage anyone from using pens to point out details.

Remember to give the photo story a title and to credit everyone involved in making it.

A photo story about family planning

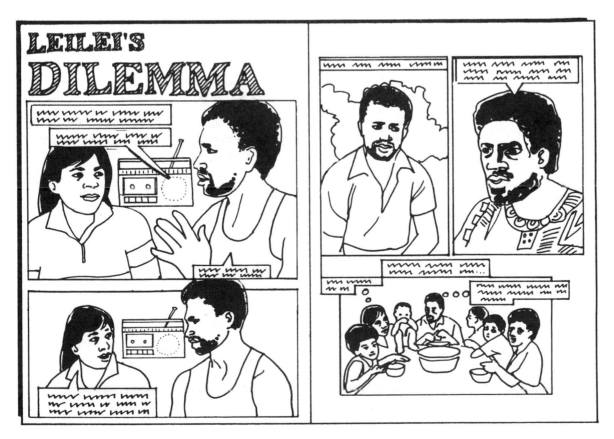

Useful tips

▶ Automatic camera users often find the difference between black- and white-skinned people makes photos very fuzzy (it can even spoil a picture of a dark-skinned person wearing a pale T-shirt). To avoid this, use fill-in flash by putting your camera onto flash mode. Be careful to change camera settings to suit the light.

▶ If the weather is overcast, your pictures can look gloomy. This problem can be solved by using a polarised filter.

▶ Inside houses or in a forested area you may find photos are too dark unless you use fill-in flash.

▶ Be aware that expensive camera equipment can be easily spoilt by heat, cold, humidity, rain, boat journeys and poor handling. Cameras do get stolen and can be hard to replace, especially if they have not been insured. One way to avoid this problem is to use so-called 'disposable' cameras (some are even waterproof) which are available in many pharmacies.

❛ There are several possible close-up shots, so decide which one you want – the basic face, head and shoulders or the whole body. The classic development photo is taken with a wide-angle lens and has a person in the foreground doing something, plus context, for example, an old man hoeing a field. Always take several pictures of 'scenes' you really want because what you've photographed may not always be what you thought you photographed. Also you may have used the wrong settings and been out of focus, though this won't happen if you are using an automatic camera. ❜
Photographer, South Africa

How to use a photo story

Photo stories are very popular in schools. They can be made by the students themselves and can be put in the class or school library. Photo stories that deal with community issues can be used with groups in development work.

4

Visual aids which summarise complex information

The visual aids in this chapter can help you to convey complex information effectively. They are ranked according to how commonly they are used and how simple they are to make, beginning with the easiest and most familiar. Remember that Chapter 1 can help you decide which visual aid to make.

All the visual aids which follow can be used in a variety of teaching and training contexts, with large or small groups. Charts, graphs and some of the calendars described can be made in less than an hour. Visual aids made of paper are easy to transport and can be made more durable by covering with clear plastic.

Maths lessons are generally where students first learn to make bar charts, line graphs and other diagrams. However, these charts can be used in other lessons, such as geography, science and language to record, evaluate and then to discuss information.

Bar chart

Bar charts are diagrams which summarise information about quantities and time in a visual way. They can be used to help people to understand quite complex information. Bar charts are made up of two types or sets of data. For example, in the bar chart on the left, rainfall per month is data set 1 and the months of the year are data set 2. The two sets of data are arranged on the graph grid to allow comparisons and conclusions to be drawn.

Bar charts can be used to show differences between many items at one time, such as the price of different items in a shopping basket.

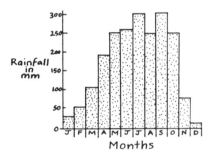

Rainfall in Uboma

The prices of food in a shopping basket

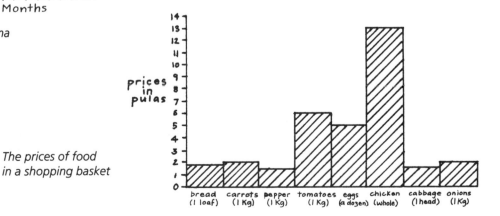

The chart above allows people to see at a glance which item is the most expensive and which item is the cheapest.

Bar charts can also show the changes in one item over a period of time, such as the difference in price of the whole shopping basket over one year.

Total price of shopping basket

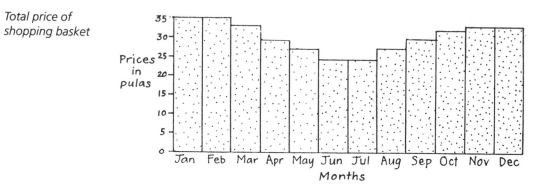

Bar charts are a useful method to teach students to use, so that they learn how to present information. For example, we had a project to measure rainfall and after discussions decided it was best to represent it with the amount of rain (shown in millimetres) on the vertical axis and the months on the horizontal axis. **9**
Maths teacher, Tanzania

The individual columns can also be divided to compare the size of the component parts which make up the total length of the column. For example, in the bar chart above showing the changes in the price of the whole shopping basket per month, the columns showing the total shopping basket could be sub-divided to show how much the individual foods cost. Such a chart would be a simple visual summary of a large amount of related information.

Bar charts can be made while the data is being collected. For example, if the class is recording the price of bananas at the end of each month, then the column for each month can be drawn as the data is recorded.

How to make a bar chart

You will need
▶ data to plot on the chart
▶ a ruler
▶ lined paper or graph paper
▶ coloured pens or crayons

What you need to do
1 Collate all the data you want to show on the bar chart.

2 Draw the axes of the graph and choose the most appropriate scales for the horizontal and vertical axes. Bar charts have vertical columns. Time is usually shown on the horizontal axis. Your scale must be appropriate for the size of the paper or chalkboard you are using. For example, if you want to show different distances ranging from 9 km to 25 km, you could use a scale of 1 cm = 1 km. However, if your distances range from 200 km to 800 km, a scale of 1 cm = 100 km would be better. All scales using numbers must start at zero.

If you do not have any graph paper, you can draw your own grid on most surfaces, including a chalkboard. Remember to put the numbers on the lines of the grid, and not in the squares.

3 Plot your data on the chart. For each division on the horizontal axis, plot the corresponding value on the vertical axis and draw a vertical column. Do this for all the data. If your chart is on graph paper, use dark or bright colours for the bars so that students can see them clearly without being confused by the grid lines on the graph paper.

4 Give the chart a title, label all the axes clearly and include a key if necessary. A key explains any abbreviations, colouring or shading you have used.

How to use bar charts

Bar charts are used to compare like with like, that is to display comparable data in a visual way that is easy to understand. They can show very simple data, as well as quite complex data, so in the classroom they can be used with both younger classes and older students. For example, primary school classes can make a bar chart which compares the number of girls and boys in the class. First count the total number of girls, and then count the total number of boys. Show the results on a bar chart where the horizontal axis shows 'girls' and 'boys', and the vertical axis has a scale for the total number. A slightly more complex chart could compare the number of brothers and sisters the pupils in the class have.

Secondary level students can use bar charts to display information in a range of subjects. For example, in agricultural science they could show the number of centimetres a crop grows each week, or in geography they could count the number of cars passing the market each hour on a given day.

CASE STUDY *Bar charts*

A primary school science class in East Africa had been recording the work that they had been doing using charts and graphs. The teacher wanted to show the pupils the need for recording information clearly, the importance of gaining the necessary skills and how to see patterns and draw conclusions from the data.

In one experiment, the students made a chart where they measured the progress of tortoises on different surfaces. When asked, some students thought that a tortoise might move faster on a rough surface than on a smooth one. They worked in pairs or groups of three and timed the movement of tortoises on a variety of surfaces. The data was then put on a chart. The teacher asked them to look at the data and draw some conclusions.

Throughout, the teacher guided the students with their work and helped them to make decisions as to which kind of chart to choose, which symbols, how wide each column should be and so on. There was a great deal of discussion about the process.

When the charts were completed, they were displayed on the wall for pupils from other classes to see. These classes asked the students questions about the data and then asked their teachers if they could carry out research and make similar charts.

In development work, bar charts can be used to summarise data about a project, both its administration and its output, for example the number of farmers participating in extension workshops each month, or the amount of money spent by the project each month.

Another important way to use bar charts in development work is to collate and display information gathered during participatory appraisals (see Calendars, pages 79–86).

Line graph

A line graph is useful to show change over a period of time, for example, the growth of a seed, the rise and fall of supply, price, quantity, etc. Sharp movements are indicated by troughs or peaks in the line. A line graph can also be used to illustrate data gathered over a long time.

Different coloured lines or lines drawn in different ways can be drawn on the same graph to compare two or more sets of data. Like bar charts, line graphs can be made as the data is collected.

How to make a line graph

You will need
► data to plot on the graph
► graph paper (or any paper)
► coloured pens or crayons
► a ruler

What you need to do

1 Collate the data you want to show on the line graph.

2 Draw the vertical and horizontal axes, decide on the scales (see Bar charts, page 68) and label them, remembering to keep the lettering horizontal. Label each point with the appropriate figure, date, number, name and so on. You may need to abbreviate names of days or months, for example.

3 Plot the points from your data, reading off each axis.

4 Join the dots with a smooth line. If the data is discontinuous – for example, you are plotting sales of maize each year – the sections of line between each point can be straight. If the data is continuous, the line should gently curve with no sharp points.

Do not make the graph too complicated, especially if it is in one colour only. More than three or four lines can be confusing – they should be clearly labelled or explained in a key.

6 There are certain conventions with graphing, so usually the time period is on the horizontal axis and the measurement on the vertical. Line graphs are great for comparing different temperatures. Each day you record the temperature and mark it with a dot. As more dots are put on the graph you can join them up. 9
Teacher trainer, Ghana

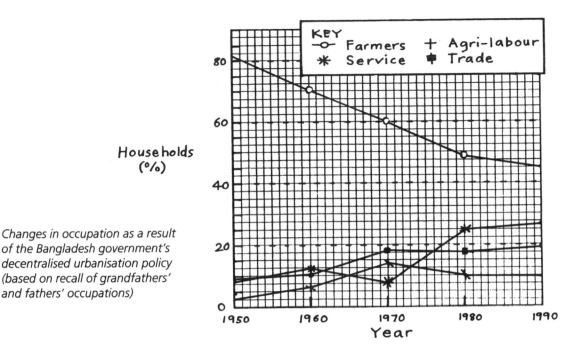

Changes in occupation as a result of the Bangladesh government's decentralised urbanisation policy (based on recall of grandfathers' and fathers' occupations)

How to use line graphs

The following is just one example of how to use a line graph in a classroom.

With your class, plant a fast-growing seed, such as a sunflower, in earth. Make sure that it is in the sun and that the students water it regularly. The students should record the height of the seedling on the same day every week.

Pie chart

A pie chart is a circle divided up into sections or wedges of different sizes by straight lines radiating out from the centre of the circle. The size of each individual section is in proportion to the total quantity of time, money or object the pie chart represents. For example, it can illustrate different sources of total annual income for a club, or activities in a 24-hour period.

Pie charts are useful with different kinds of group and all types of learner. They can be used for teaching, training and working with communities.

How to make a pie chart

You will need
► data for the pie chart
► paper
► coloured pens or crayons
► a ruler
► string
► a pin
► a pencil

You can also draw the pie chart on a chalkboard, whiteboard or flipchart.

If you have a computer, many software packages contain a graphics option which generates pie charts from numerical data.

What you need to do

1 Draw a circle. Follow the instructions on how to draw a circle in Chapter 6, page 107. The centre of the circle is where the pin marks the paper.

2 Lie another piece of string around the edge of the circle and then cut it to exactly the length of the circle's circumference.

3 Calculate the fraction or percentage of each component to be shown as a section of the circle. For example, let us say that the string is 20 cm long. The total income of a sewing club is $100. This is represented by the string which is 20 cm long. The income from selling shirts is $15 which is 15% of the total income. Find 15% of the length of the string by calculating 15% × 20 cm = 3 cm. Mark the string 3 cm from one end. Then calculate the percentage for each of the other components in the same way, and mark the string accordingly.

4 Lie the string around the circle again and each of the marks will show where to draw lines from the edge of the circle to the centre, dividing it into sections. Each section will then represent the relative importance of different sources of income for the sewing club.

Pie chart

1. Draw the circle
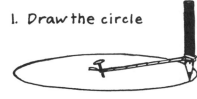

2. Cut a piece of string the length of the edge of the circle.
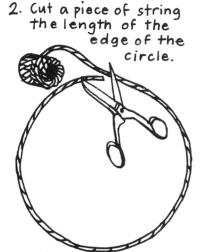

3. Measure off the percentage of each section.
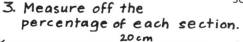

Selling shirts ($15)
Selling skirts and dresses ($45)
Rental of building ($5)
Refreshment sales ($10)
Selling screen-printed shorts ($25)

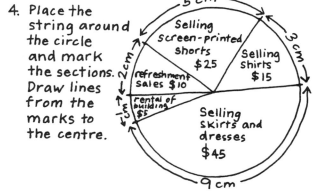

4. Place the string around the circle and mark the sections. Draw lines from the marks to the centre.

Selling screen-printed shorts $25
Selling shirts $15
refreshment sales $10
rental of building $5
Selling skirts and dresses $45

5 Draw in the sections and label them. You could also colour each one and explain the colours in a key. Remember to give the chart a title to explain what it shows.

Always check that the students or trainees understand the information presented.

Like all visual aids, pie charts can be made with or by students or communities. The example below illustrates the changes in crop production of farmers in Ethiopia after resettlement. After a demonstration by the development workers, two literate farmers drew them.

❝ A good way of demonstrating where an amount of money is going, say a country's gross national production (GNP) or the costs of a sewing group, is to draw a circle and then using the figures you have, divide the circle into slices of pie. ❞
Teacher trainer, Ghana

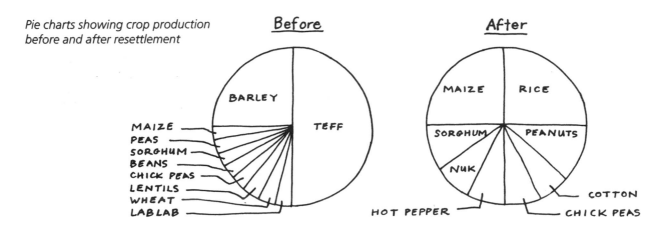

Pie charts showing crop production before and after resettlement

In this case the pie chart was called an *enjera* (a local circular, cereal-based dish) and the central point and sections were drawn freehand to show the rough proportions of different crops.

Map

A map is a flat drawing or representation of an area, such as a village, which shows the location of natural and man-made features and resources. A map is drawn or made to be smaller than real life, and is not always to scale.

In development work, a village or community map made by learners or participants in a project can serve a number of purposes. Communities can think about what resources they lack and plan the most suitable place to build new resources, such as a well or a school. Mapping can help outsiders to become more familiar with an area and with the people who live there. The process of making a map can encourage co-operation between people, by jointly assessing their situation and needs. By using and valuing their own knowledge and perceptions, people may feel encouraged to take action to solve their problems.

Maps drawn by different groups of people in a community, for example by groups of young and old people, or by people of different ethnic and cultural backgrounds, will reflect differences in their perceptions, priorities and needs. This may have important consequences for the success of a project. If one group includes features that another group excludes, this may reveal inequalities in access to and ownership of resources such as firewood, water, land or institutions, such as schools and shops.

❻ Men and women in north-west Pakistan were asked to draw a map of their village showing where they wanted new handpumps to be installed. The men marked sites near the mosque and the bazaar (where women rarely go). The women, who have primary responsibility for collecting water daily for household use, selected sites near their houses, but which were not in view of public places like the tea shop. If only the men had been

consulted, the new water supply would have been inappropriately located and would not have had the desired impact of improving health and hygiene and reducing drudgery, because women would have been reluctant to use the new handpumps. 9
Community development worker, Pakistan

Maps can be made to show what an area looked like in the past, or to show how a community would like it to look in the future.

Social mapping is a way of showing on a map all households in a community. This can help to identify the poorer members of a community, or where different groups live.

However, it is important to be aware that there may be places which are associated with local traditions and religious or cultural practices which villagers may be reluctant to tell outsiders about.

6 Cultural beliefs determined the kind of information that was shown on the map. For example, the initial maps did not show the position of waterholes and places of initiation until I settled in the village and some kind of trust was established.9
Demographer, Zimbabwe

Maps made by students or communities may take several days or weeks to build up, as they gain confidence through the process. Leave any map with the group you have made it with. If you want to keep a copy, make your own or take photographs.

Making a map in a classroom can help to teach students about the concept of maps and how to interpret them. It can help the students to reflect on their own surroundings. For example, they might make a map of the health and safety hazards in the school compound, village or town, showing features such as busy roads, blind corners, unprotected water sources, rubbish tips and stagnant ponds where mosquitoes breed. This might be part of a project to protect the environment or to campaign for road safety measures.

How to make a floor map

6 I often drew in the dust because it was convenient and to hand – and particularly good for explaining where something was. 9
In-service teacher trainer, Zanzibar

A floor map can be drawn in dust or mud, drawn with chalk onto a cement floor, or drawn on a large sheet of paper on the floor. Houses, roads and other features can be marked with stones, seeds and so on.

You will need
- ▶ chalk or a stick
- ▶ objects to make the features of the village, such as sticks, stones, leaves or fruit
- ▶ a flat area with plenty of space which will not be disturbed – it may be concrete, dust or mud
- ▶ pen and paper to copy the village map yourself, or a camera

What you need to do
In development work, ask the participants to draw their village or surrounding area on the ground, or on a large piece of paper. Encourage them to think of all the features and resources they see and use, and to draw them or represent them with the objects. You could suggest they start by walking around the village or area.

Women's map

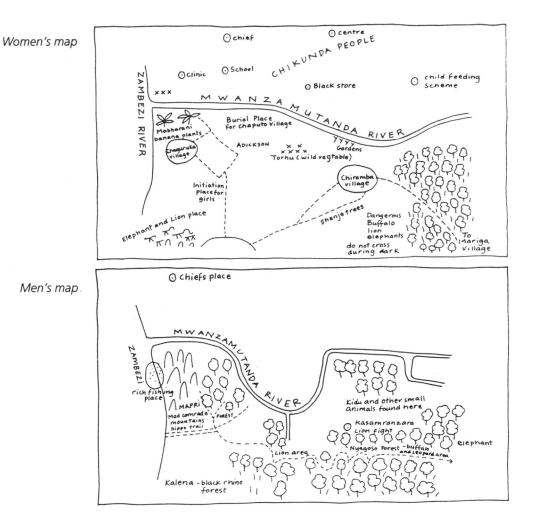

Men's map.

The examples above show how the men and women of Tembomvura drew two different maps of their village. The men's map shows the area as it was in the past, with hunting areas marked. The women's map shows the village as it is now, with key institutions such as the school, clinic and child feeding scheme marked. This mapping exercise was useful because it indicated gender differences in the community.

However, if the purpose of the map is to provide the most comprehensive and accurate representation of an area, a range of informants should be consulted to check the information contained in a map.

Making maps in the classroom can often form part of project work in many subjects, including biology, geography and environmental science. To make a map of health and safety hazards, for example, groups or pairs of students can go on a walk to collect data for the map. Each group or pair could visit a different part of the school or village, make rough sketches and note any health hazards they see and where they are located. When they get back to the classroom, the map can be made.

How to make a wall map

A wall map is a flat representation of all or part of the earth's surface showing the natural and man-made features, such as rivers and cities. It can be hung on a wall and is useful in classrooms or other formal teaching settings. Wall maps can be purchased ready-printed.

Maps of individual countries, regions or districts are usually available from tourist, airline and government offices. Maps that need to be kept for future use should be rolled up and stored in a dry place.

You will need
▶ large sheets of paper or card
▶ coloured pens or crayons

What you need to do

1 Draw the outline of the map on a large sheet of strong paper or card (see Templates, pages 117–118).

2 Mark the position of important places (for example, use dots to mark the position of towns and villages). Print the names of the places on small pieces of coloured card. Put these horizontally on the map so that they are easy to read. Include essential information, but make sure you do not overcrowd the map.

How to make a three-dimensional map

A three-dimensional map is a model which shows the contours, the height and depth of features, both natural and man-made, of an area.

If you are not experienced in making this type of map, ask the arts and crafts teacher for assistance.

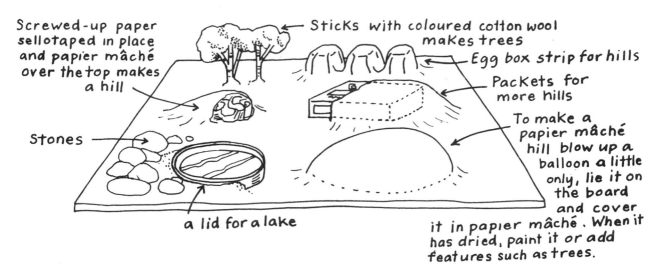

Screwed-up paper sellotaped in place and papier mâché over the top makes a hill

Sticks with coloured cotton wool makes trees

Egg box strip for hills

Packets for more hills

Stones

To make a papier mâché hill blow up a balloon a little only, lie it on the board and cover it in papier mâché. When it has dried, paint it or add features such as trees.

a lid for a lake

You will need
▶ a piece of plywood or linoleum to form the base of the map
▶ a variety of different materials to make the features on the map – paper, cardboard, egg boxes, foil, tin lids, bottle tops and caps, cloth, matchboxes, shells, stones, sand, paint, wood shavings and so on
▶ papier mâché (see Chapter 6, pages 113–114)

The students or trainees can ask local shopkeepers and artisans for junk and remnants of any materials they use. Everything needs to be stored in separate boxes and bags, and labelled.

What you need to do
1 Make a base for the map by cutting a large square or rectangle from a piece of plywood or linoleum.

2 Ask the students or trainees to discuss the relief map they want. You can provide information and/or resources where needed.

3 Make a rough sketch to show the position of all the features to be included (for example, where the river flows, hills, houses, and so on).

If the students want the model to be roughly to scale, make a simple sketch of the features on squared graph paper of the same size as the plywood base.

Give each sketched figure an appropriate size when compared with another feature, so that, for instance, the houses are smaller than the hill, the river is narrower than the hill, and so on. Use the sketch as a guide for the papier mâché features.

The students might also want to mark the compass points – north, south, east, west – on the model.

4 Make the papier mâché (see Chapter 6, pages 113–114).

5 Use the papier mâché to create landscape features on the base board, for example, a mound to make a mountain. You can paint and varnish these as you wish.

❛ Papier mâché is especially good for the background of a 3-D map. A landscape can be made with unwanted packets or built up with newspaper. Use twigs for trees and stones for rocks. An egg box strip doubles for hills, a blown up balloon with papier mâché pasted over can make a mound. Screwed up paper sellotaped in place and then covered with papier mâché makes a hill, while a lid can make a good lake, especially if you put stones and sand around its edge. ❜
Art and craft teacher, Bhutan

6 The students can then add the other features, following their planned layout, using the materials they have collected, such as twigs for trees, ribbon for rivers, and so on.

Encourage the students to keep the map as simple as possible.

Floors and the ground as visual aids

Floors made of earth, sand, mud and concrete can make excellent bases for visual aids. They are particularly useful if there are no large sheets of paper available, or if the local people are not comfortable using paper and pens. Using the ground can also ensure that the class or large group (or community) is able to see and contribute to the teaching, training or participatory session.

You should ask permission before marking floors.

A group of Indian men producing a map on the ground, using stones, seeds, sticks and sand to represent features and buildings

❝ We asked people to chart the foods which they used to eat and foods they ate now. In one row people put foods – green banana, mango, pawpaw, cabbage and egg as well as symbols (like a pebble or the shape scratched in the soil) for chicken and goat meat. People then discussed how their diet had changed. ❞
Community adviser, Uganda

You will need
▶ a concrete or compacted dirt floor
▶ chalk, charcoal, a burnt stick or a sharp stick with which to mark the floor

To make a written record you will also need
▶ paper
▶ pens

You can use the floor and other surfaces to illustrate the design of a particular building.

❝ It was a problem finding enough pegs to mark out building plans. But it was important the students learnt how to mark out awkwardly-shaped buildings, and not just the square ones. Even if the students did spend time finding pegs, the ground was usually so hard it was difficult to knock them into the soil. Instead the students used to draw out plans to scale using chalk on the workshop floor. It was a lot quicker and a lot cooler! Afterwards they'd copy the designs into their notebooks. ❞
Building instructor, Kenya

Dry ground

Dry ground is good when you are working with a large group because you don't need any special equipment. It is particularly good for displaying commonly used, grown or eaten products when discussing nutrition.

Sand and wet ground (mud)

❝ During a health workshop in a very rural area I was playing with a stick in the sand. One of the women from the clinic came up to me and said 'I do that! I always draw my health education stories in the sand'. ❞
Graphic designer, Namibia

Damp sand and mud are excellent for drawing on because they can hold an indent which is more visual than lines on a flat piece of concrete. You can also erase mistakes and re-draw easily. A sharp stick is effective as a writing tool.

Sand is especially useful if you want to clarify points when building something from a design.

❝ During the nitty-gritty of making a cage, I would draw a diagram (almost a pattern) of a cage on the sand. Sometimes the villagers would draw the design. The idea was to check that the message was clear. You must do that, especially if you are explaining the same information to different villages, as it is easy to forget the problems you faced when first learning about the design process. ❞
Coastal aquaculture development officer, Solomon Islands

When students are learning to write, sand is extremely useful for them to learn how to form the letters and then words. They can also draw pictures in the sand to match the words they write.

Calendar

A calendar is a symbolic representation of events over a period of time. Making a calendar, such as a seasonal calendar, with a community is a development technique for collecting data. That data can then be displayed as a bar chart or line graph.

A wide variety of calendars, like the time trend or events calendar, are used by teachers and participatory approach practitioners working with communities. These approaches may appear simple. However, they need a great deal of preparation. You also need to develop trust between yourself and the local people. It is important that the teacher or trainer is aware that the purpose of this process is for the local people to reveal their concerns. These concerns may prove to be very different from those that were anticipated. (For more information about participatory techniques see page 7.)

In primary schools, calendars can be made by the students to show the days of the week and the months of the year. The students can write in their birthdays and important festivals. In secondary school, the students can make calendars in geography, agricultural science or hygiene lessons, for example. Local communities can make calendars to record the changing features of their lives over a period of time.

There are several types of calendar:
► weather calendar
► seasonal calendar
► time trend, or events, calendar

How to make a weather calendar (for primary schools)

You will need
► two large sheets of white card or strong paper
► a pencil or pen and crayons
► a ruler

What you need to do

1 Draw fourteen large squares on the card: seven on the top and seven on the bottom. Write Sunday, Monday, and so on in the squares on the top.

2 On the side of the paper write 'Morning' next to the top squares and 'Afternoon' next to the bottom squares.

3 Draw symbols for each type of weather on a separate piece of paper as a key. Use symbols the students will recognise, such as a yellow circle with rays coming from it for the sun.

How to use a weather calendar

The children observe the weather in the morning and the afternoon every day of a given week. They can take it in turns to draw in the correct symbol in the appropriate square.

	Sunday	Monday	Tuesday	Wednesday	Thursday	Friday	Saturday
Morning							
Afternoon							

This weekly calendar can be used to collect different types of information. If you want to make a monthly calendar, draw up a chart with thirty-one squares.

How to make a seasonal calendar (for secondary schools and development work)

A seasonal calendar is a visual record of the main activities and events which happen during the year for an individual, a household, a school or a community.

In development work, a seasonal calendar can be used to summarise all or some of the things that have an impact on people's lives. It can help to build up research knowledge about an area, especially if there is little formal data, and to identify problems and opportunities for solving problems. A seasonal calendar can show the times of the year when people face the greatest difficulty, for example when food is the most scarce just before the main harvest, or perhaps when sections of the community are not so busy and could engage in income-generating activities.

Seasonal calendars can contain information about the following:
▶ climate (rainfall and temperature)
▶ cropping patterns
▶ human diseases (when they occur and when they are most serious)
▶ livestock breeding, feeding and management activities and disease patterns
▶ crop pests and diseases
▶ labour demand for men, women and children
▶ fluctuations in prices of staple goods and times of greatest debt
▶ social and religious events and ceremonies
▶ diet changes and food shortages/surpluses
▶ water sources used at different times of the year.

When making a seasonal calendar, remember that some of the data collected, such as rainfall and temperature, will be relative and not absolute. For example, if a village is recording rainfall patterns on a seasonal calendar, the data may show quite clearly that in December it rains much more than in July. It will not, however, show the actual amount it rained each month. A seasonal calendar enables valid comparisons to be made without the need for accurate, formal statistics which are often not available. Seasonal calendars usually show eighteen months of data because a twelve-month calendar will not reveal the full cycle of seasonal patterns such as planting and harvesting.

You will need
▶ large sheets of paper or card
▶ pens
▶ a checklist of questions based on preliminary discussions, observations and a review of secondary data

What you need to do

1 Ask people to gather round in a semi-circle, and ask someone to draw a long, horizontal axis on a large piece of paper, or on the ground. Alternatively, you could use a stick or bamboo for the axis.

2 Mark divisions on the axis, for example, months or years.

3 If, for example, you wanted the calendar to show rainfall patterns from month to month, you can use columns of seeds or pebbles placed along the axis to show the relative amounts of rainfall each month. Agricultural activities can be shown using the appropriate materials (such as coffee beans to indicate when coffee is planted and harvested), but this can become complex.

6 To examine the prevalence of particular diseases during certain seasons, the groups were asked to rank each disease on a scale of one to ten (using seeds), according to the frequency of occurrence of the disease during a particular season. The information was used to design a local seasonal disease calendar. 9
Demographer, Zimbabwe

Verbal cross-checking can take place at the end of the exercise. Different groups do have different responsibilities and roles, so it is important to enable all community members to contribute their views in order to gain a comprehensive picture. For example, if you are planning a health project, consult older people and children because they are more vulnerable to disease and fall ill more often than young and middle-aged adults.

Seasonal calendars can be made in a school setting to explore a specific topic, such as weather changes over the year, and to collect data to be used for making bar charts.

The following guidelines will help you to collect data for different seasonal calendars.

Rainfall

To find out about rainfall patterns, you can ask farmers for the estimates of the number of days of rainfall per month in a 'normal' year. Alternatively, you can ask which is the wettest month, the next wettest, the dryest and so on, to build up a picture.

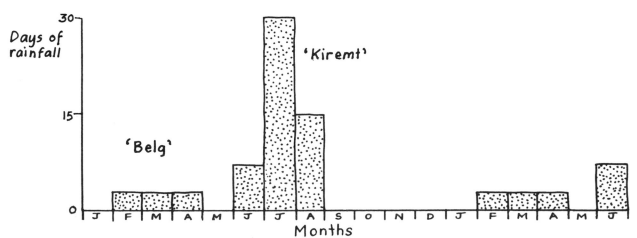

Rainfall calendar, Abicho, Ethiopia

However, the use of months as a time period may not be appropriate. In this case, establish key events (religious festivals, traditional ceremonies, and so on) to gauge the time of year being discussed. Then cross-check against secondary data (that is, government metereological statistics, etc., for the area).

Leave the original calendar with the people who made it. For your own records, take slides or photographs and make a copy in your notebook. Large versions can be prepared on paper for presenting to the school and/or community to check whether they agree with the interpretation placed on their answers and discussions.

Crop patterns

You can ask when crops are planted and harvested and also find out the relative importance of each crop. This can be shown by building up vertical columns of seeds, for example, in relation to the relative size of the crop (the horizontal length spans the months that a particular crop is under cultivation). Common pests and plant diseases can be recorded in this way too, according to when they are most prevalent and destructive, and which crops are most affected. Rainfed and irrigated crops can be documented separately.

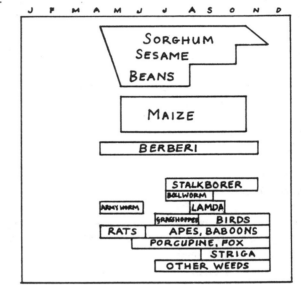

Rainfed crop calendar, Abicho, Ethiopia

Labour demand

First, ask which month has the highest labour requirement, the next highest, and so on, for the four busiest months. Then ask which month requires the lowest amount of labour, then the next lowest, and so on (the four quietest months). For the remaining months, ask the farmers to compare them to each other, two months at a time. Discuss the final diagram and ask them to correct any mistakes.

Further detail can be obtained by establishing activity calendars for agricultural and non-agricultural activities. It is very important that this type of calendar drawing exercise is carried out with men, women and children, and with different socio-economic groups in the village. In this way you will be able to establish how labour constraints and surpluses affect people differently. It is vital to ensure that development interventions do not make assumptions about the availability of labour for community projects. For example, if women are working hard weeding and hoeing crops at

In a village in Ghana, villagers felt angry that the Ministry of Agriculture seemed to have ignored requests to come and help them improve their cash crops. The last cocoa crop had been very poor. When an agricultural extension officer went home on leave, he saw that the problem was not just about crop yields. There was too little fertile ground close to the village and there were many more people living in the area than ten years before.

The extension officer had attended a workshop where he had been shown how participatory rural appraisal (PRA) techniques could be used. After discussion with his family and some of the elders he thought the approach might work well at his village.

Organising a PRA visit took a long time, but because the agricultural extension officer had explained the process to the leaders in the village, the villagers were pleased when the team arrived. There were several 'experts' from the city and overseas in the team. Instead of going on a walk through the village and plantations, handing over crop medicines and leaving before dusk, the outsiders introduced themselves and sat down and talked. They asked when people in the village were less busy, and suggested that this would be the best time to have their first meeting.

It was night time when the first mapping session was held and nearly everyone from the village was there. There was some light from the moon, but kerosene lights were also being used. One of the visitors asked if someone would mark the village road by scratching its course using a stick. Then everyone was asked to mark their houses. The first few used the stick, making a cross mark on the dusty ground, but it was hard for everyone to see. One old woman joked they should use stones for the houses and seeds for the kitchens. Everyone laughed but decided it was a good idea. Then someone suggested the church should be put on the map, another person wanted the school building marked out, and another their copra shed…

Gradually a really good map of the area was made showing every house, kitchen, animal shed, water source, path and field. To a stranger it would have just looked like a drawing on the ground with lots of leaves, fruits, nuts, shells and twigs crossing it.

Over the next few weeks the villagers spent many hours talking with the extension workers. They created seasonal calendars and other diagrams to show the patterns of cocoa growing, agricultural and non-agricultural work, and the timing of the work needed in the cocoa plantations.

Once the villagers started to discuss the final calendar, they realised that although they had known about some problems which affected the poor cocoa crop, there were in fact other factors which were related but which, until then, had not been considered a part of the problem. There were three main problems with the cocoa crop: at the time the cocoa plantations needed most work, the men were working in the nearby town and had no time to cultivate the cash crop, the women were too busy in their own vegetable and food gardens and could not spare the time to walk the five miles to the cocoa plantation and back every day, and lastly that the dispute over payment for the fertiliser and pesticides for the cocoa crop meant that these had not been bought.

It was clear that they could not solve all of these problems – the men needed the money from the work in town at that time of the year and the cocoa plantation could not be moved closer to the village, because there was no fertile land available there. The older women in the village wanted to form groups and start small businesses, selling some of their vegetable produce and the baskets that most older women weave in the evenings, in order to supplement the family cash income. Although the women did not know how they would be able to get the money to start these projects, this idea was well-received.

The extension officer knew that an aid agency supported community-based income-generating projects and the village head and two older village women went to negotiate a small start-up loan. After one year, the women had used the loan to start their income-generation activities, and with part of their proceeds had set up a credit and savings scheme. The problems with the cocoa crop were not solved as a result of this participatory activity, but the extra income which the women are earning has benefitted their families.

a time of year when men are not engaged in any activity, the introduction of a project which would depend on women (for example, food processing) would increase the burden on women, while doing nothing to address the problem of seasonal male unemployment.

Diet

Ask what food is normally eaten and how many meals are consumed. Then ask if the number of meals are ever reduced and, if so, when. Ask which foods, if any, are not available at certain times of the year. It is important to gauge differences between members of one household, as well as between households themselves.

Health

Diseases and their seasonal variations can be established by asking when, for example, malaria and diarrhoea are most severe. This can be either according to month, rainfall or farm activity. Bar charts can then be used to illustrate this information.

Finally, all the components of the seasonal calendar can be collated by students in the classroom or with the participation of the community in development work. Their local situation can then be analysed. This can be the starting point for action to be taken by the students and/or the community if required, for example, draining stagnant pools before the rainy season to prevent malaria.

How to make a time trend calendar

6 An events calendar is a widely used way of trying to find the ages of children. 9
Doctor, Kenya

A time trend calendar (also called an events calendar) aims to record major events and to help establish a record of changes over time. Use time trends to record historical differences, for example, environmental changes, choice of crops or staple diet. Talking with the older generation in a village is an extremely useful method of finding information in order to develop a time trend. Students could interview the elders for such a project.

You will need
- ▶ flat ground or floor
- ▶ objects to represent events (stones, and so on)
- ▶ paper and pens for making a permanent copy

What you need to do

1 Mark a horizontal or vertical axis on the ground. Divide it into equal sections, each one representing a year.

2 Build up an historical profile by asking people whether, for example, certain crops were being cultivated when a typhoon or other major natural disaster occurred.

Use secondary data and records of important events or dates marked on buildings as reference points. Ask questions, such as, 'Did this start before the school, clinic, and so on, was built or afterwards?'

?	Original forest cut
1860	Kates village is established
1938	20 houses
1942	45 houses
1945	All teak already cut by farmers during WW II
1962	Land reform by Agraria
1962/3	All durian trees already cut down
1967	Replanting of teak by Perum Perhutani
1969	Typhoon - subsequent cutting of trees surrounding houses
1976	Extension began for tegal and Sawah on fertilizers, pesticides
1977	Introduction of orange trees and ceramic production began
1978	Dissemination of Kaliandra/Elephant grass regreening seeds from Kabupaten
1979	Introduction of Clove trees
1980	Transmigration
1981	Off-farm 'Konveksi' work began
1983	Transmigration
1985	Introduction of UPSA regreening experiment; Check dam constructed
1987	867 houses; introduction of UACP

Time trend calendar for a village in East Java

3 Mark the events on the axis using different objects to represent different events, or types of event.

4 For an accurate record, check information with as many informants as possible.

Flow diagram

Flow diagrams show successive movements step-by-step through a process from start to finish. They can be used to explain processes, such as how to make water safe to drink. They can be useful to students or communities to analyse the causes and effects of problems, and to suggest solutions (when they may also be called problem and objective trees). Flow diagrams record inter-connections, knock-on effects and help find the root cause of particular problems.

Flow diagrams can be made by students or by trainees during a group training session. They need to be pre-tested rigorously before being presented.

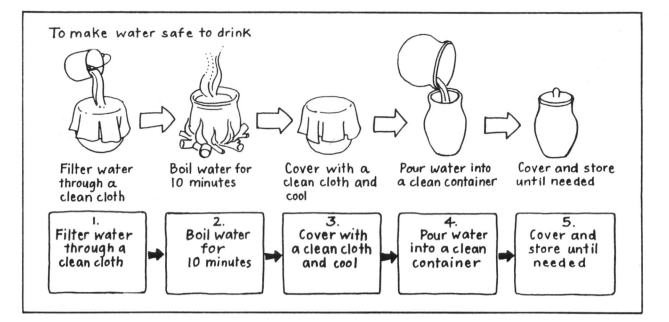

To make water safe to drink

| 1. Filter water through a clean cloth | 2. Boil water for 10 minutes | 3. Cover with a clean cloth and cool | 4. Pour water into a clean container | 5. Cover and store until needed |

How to make a flow diagram

You will need

▶ paper

▶ pens

▶ a checklist of questions to ask about a process or a problem

What you need to do

1 To make a flow diagram to show a process, decide what the main stages of the process are.

2 Write down or draw the main stages in sequence and draw a box around each one.

3 Show how the stages are linked by using a system that is easily understood by the local people. You might choose arrows to join the boxes, or possibly number each box in sequence.

4 Pre-test the diagram with local people to make sure it is accurate and that it will be understood. Make any changes necessary. Pre-testing is essential for processes which may involve risks to people's safety if misunderstood.

5
Visual aids for activities

The visual aids in this chapter are props to use in learning activities. Those which are easiest to make and most commonly used are given first. Chapter 1 will help you decide which is best for your purpose.

All the visual aids in this chapter can be used indoors or outdoors. Most are suitable for large or small groups; however, if you are using a model with a large group, you may need to make more than one so that everyone can have a turn at looking at or using it. With games, you will need extra sets of cards and boards if many players are to be involved.

Plays, puppets, masks, models and pocket charts can be used with people who are literate or non-literate. They are extremely popular with children.

All the visual aids in this chapter are particularly useful for communication activities in language classes. The students can write their own plays and make the puppets in art and craft classes. Some of the card and board games help to improve their spelling too. Card games, pocket charts, models, and finger puppets are the quickest visual aids to make in this chapter.

Card games

Card games can be useful in the classroom to consolidate learning, as well as in development work to reinforce a particular message, for example in health and nutrition. In both cases they can stimulate discussion.

It is important to make the matching cards as similar as possible, otherwise the players may be confused.

> ❛ I handed out two plain bits of same sized card to each member of the group. They then drew two picture cards with the same food on it, for example an apricot or dhal, so we soon had a complete set of playing cards and were able to play 'Pairs'. We could also use these cards to discuss which were body-building foods, which were energy foods and so on. ❜
> *Community worker, Pakistan*

How to make a card game

You will need
► duplicate pictures from magazines or drawings of a similar size
► strong card
► coloured pens

What you need to do
Either stick the magazine pictures onto card or draw the pictures on the card.

For language lessons you can either write words underneath both the pictures, on just one of the matching pictures, or alternatively on separate pieces of card.

How to use a card game

In language lessons in primary school you can use a set of picture cards and a set of word cards in the following way. Hold up a card so the students can name the picture. Then point to the matching word on a separate card and ask them to read the word. You can then ask for volunteers to come out and match the word to the correct picture.

Divide the class into groups and give each group a set of picture and a set of word cards. Now they can play Pairs.

To play Pairs: The players spread all the cards out face downwards. The first player chooses two cards. If they match the player keeps the pair. If they do not match, the player puts the cards back face downwards. Then the next player takes two, and so on. The winner is the player who has the most pairs when there are no more cards left. The object of the game is for the players to remember which picture/word card is where. It is a game of memory as well as language learning. The players could also say the word when they turn a card face upwards. This helps their reading skills.

Pocket chart

A pocket chart is a wall chart which has a number of 'pockets' made of card glued onto it. Pictures can be displayed on the front of the pocket and pieces of paper can be inserted into the pockets. The whole chart can be carried around from place to place, rolled up if necessary.

Pocket charts can enable people to see the different types of initiative on offer in a development project and to choose which one they prefer. For example, a pocket chart with five pockets could be pinned up on a community building wall and could show five different types of water pump which could be built. After studying the different pictures, individuals then vote for the water pump they think is most suitable, by placing a piece of paper in the pocket showing that water pump.

In development work, pocket charts are useful tools for gathering information and opinions. They are particularly useful in appraising projects and in monitoring and evaluation work. For example, they can enable a group of people to register their individual opinions about a potential project, as above.

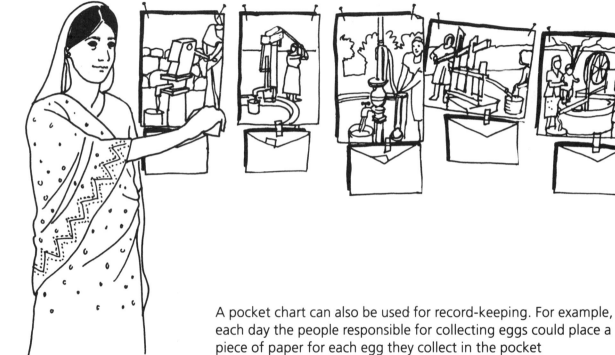

6 Because voting with the pocket chart is an individual activity it enables the shyest members...to have a voice. 9
Workshop facilitator, Tanzania

A pocket chart can also be used for record-keeping. For example, each day the people responsible for collecting eggs could place a piece of paper for each egg they collect in the pocket corresponding to that day of the week (it will be necessary to decide how the different days will be distinguished, for example a different colour pocket could be used for each day of the week).

If you need to compare and evaluate different activities then display two picture pocket charts, and the students or local people can then place their individual votes into the relevant envelope.

How to make a pocket chart

You will need
- ▶ large envelopes
- ▶ photographs or pictures which depict current practices or potential choices, for example, a planned water supply
- ▶ pieces of paper for 'voting'

What you need to do

1 Pin or stick the pictures or photographs in a line on the wall.

2 Attach an envelope to each picture.

3 Have the pieces of paper nearby for voting.

How to use a pocket chart

Explain to the students or participants what the pocket chart is for. Emphasise that voting needs to be confidential. Then have a 'dress rehearsal'. In private each person looks at the pictures and places their 'voting slip' inside their chosen envelope. Discuss with the students or the trainees how the voting can be kept confidential and how to avoid voters being influenced.

At the end of the real voting session, ask for some volunteers to take the votes out of the envelopes and count them. When the counting is finished, evaluate the results, for example, why have so many voted for this option?

Finally, the implications for the future can be discussed in the light of the results.

When the procedure has been completed, leave the pocket charts with the students or the participants. You can take a photograph of the pocket chart in use and keep a record of the results.

Masks

Masks cover and disguise the face. They can represent different characters, people, animals, and even objects. They are excellent for plays, role-plays and so on, especially when the masks represent a widely-recognised character. When using masks, a practised skit (short, satirical sketch) can clarify an educational campaign, provide information, or simply be played for amusement. To enforce a healthy eating campaign, for example, you could use masks of different foods (also see puppets page 96).

When the masks are not being used, either hang them up as a colourful display or place them in a clearly labelled, strong box.

❛ Masks...gave added impact to the message enacted by the theatre group. For example, we worked out a short play about logging. During a logging workshop, the facilitators would discuss the pros and cons of logging with villagers, then at night the acting team would put on the play, which was always enjoyed by all ages. The following day the workshop facilitators usually distributed a comic book version of the logging play. The story involved a bird from overseas that turned up in the village one day and promised it would excrete pure gold and make everybody rich if it was fed logs. The bird, of course, flew off when the trees ran out and the villagers suffered great hardship.

We found the best way to make one of the actors look like a bird was by using a mask with a beak! 9
Community theatre trainer, Solomon Islands

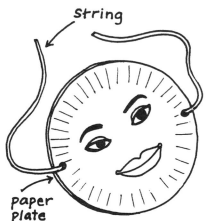

How to make a mask

You will need
- ▶ shaped cardboard (for example, cereal packets, paper plates)
- ▶ scissors
- ▶ glue
- ▶ string or strong thread
- ▶ wool or other material
- ▶ coloured pencils or paints

What you need to do

1 Draw a face on the shaped cardboard to represent the character you want. Colour it in using paint, coloured pencils or material. You could use wool for the hair.

2 Cut out holes for the eyes and the mouth. Make sure they are in the correct place for the person who is going to wear the mask.

3 Make a small hole at either side of the mask at the same level as the eyes.

4 Thread string or strong thread through the small holes. Knot it on the front of the mask. It can then be tied around the person's head to hold the mask in place.

How to use masks in plays

The advantage of plays is that they can convey a teaching or training message in an enjoyable way to audiences of different educational standards and ages. Discussing a play is also a useful stimulus for starting a debate on certain issues. A play does not have to be long to convey a clear message.

When choosing a play, ask advice from other teachers, NGOs or national acting groups. Props will make a play seem more real. If the play is being performed in an isolated rural area, use objects which are available locally as props. However, you may need to provide some items (for example, condoms for a play about AIDS), if they are essential for the understanding of the play. Some health messages may be controversial in your area, so check that the props you intend to use will not cause offence.

Models and toys

A model is a three-dimensional copy of an object, person or structure, such as a house or latrine. It is usually smaller in scale than the original and simplified. Models are valuable teaching and training aids in both the classroom and development work. They can be used to teach a skill or to illustrate a teaching point in a realistic way. Learning by doing is the most effective way of learning and if resources are limited or making mistakes may have serious consequences, using a model means the participants can practise the task. For example, some livestock students were introduced to butchering with a life-size model of a goat made of papier mâché. Chalk lines were drawn on it to show the different cuts of meat and, although the papier mâché model took some time to make, it was used again and again by many different groups – and, unlike a real animal, it stayed still.

For pre-primary and primary children, models are often toys. Toys play an important part in the development of children of all abilities: they stimulate play, develop co-ordination and intellectual abilities.

The actual process of making a model with a group of students or adult participants can also be a valuable teaching or training tool.

6 One exercise I used involved asking a group to work together as a team on a particular task. It's a simulation exercise and then you apply it to a particular situation which the group is all involved in, like a women's group doing an income-generation project which may not be working as anticipated. I'd show the group a model which I'd built with all sorts of rubbish, including Coke, Fanta and Tusker beer bottle tops, and then they'd have to make their own model. As they do it you can see who's bossing whom, who is withdrawing, which people are getting involved and how arguments develop. Then I would talk about what happened with the group and ask if that's what happened when they were selling their bread. The exercise helps the group look at its own dynamic. 9
Community worker, Kenya

6 The local pottery made models and toys to my design, and then made a good profit on the other copies they made and sold! 9
Speech therapist, Nepal

Models can be made from materials like clay and dough, from papier mâché, or with a little imagination they can be made from whatever materials are available and can be collected locally. You can also ask local craftsmen such as potters, carpenters and car mechanics if they can make or copy designs for you.

How to make clay, mud or dough models

In some countries children are skilled at modelling from mud and make copies of many things including people, animals, food and so on. They therefore also know where to find the best mud for modelling.

You will need
► clay, mud or dough (which can be shaped and then baked and varnished or painted)
► paint and/or varnish
► access to a kiln (potter's oven) or other suitable oven

See Chapter 6, page 104 for instructions on making dough.

What you need to do
1 Form the model by hand while the material is soft.

2 Leave it to harden or fire (bake) it in a kiln or other oven.

3 Once it has dried or been fired, the model can be painted with thick paint and/or varnished.

How to make junk models

You will need
► any clean, unwanted objects such as cloth, bottle tops, cardboard, etc.
► any natural materials such as twigs, leaves, shells, seeds, etc.
► glue (some glue may not stick all the materials together, so you could also use parcel tape, masking tape or sticky tape)
► paint and/or varnish

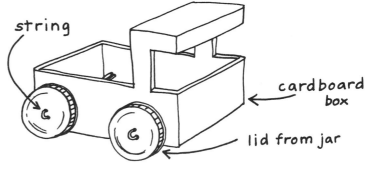

string

cardboard box

lid from jar

❝ Junk models are especially good for buildings and human or animal figures. Any kind of box, plastic container, straw, material and scraps can be used. A folded carton can be used for a house roof, to make wheels move put lids onto an axle made from a twig or bamboo. Parts of a junk model can be painted or wax-crayoned, but tin or plastic surfaces need to be covered with paper first unless you find an oil-based paint. ❞
Art and craft teacher, Bhutan

How to use models and toys

All models and toys are excellent teaching and training aids in the classroom and for development work, and with literate and non-literate participants. They are particularly valuable for demonstrations and simulations, where the teacher or trainer uses a model to show the learners how a task or process is carried out. The trainees watch and then try to carry out the task themselves.

Most livestock problems faced by a women's group in Nepal arose because the animals were not given enough fodder. A livestock development officer in Nepal and her colleague discussed ways in which they could demonstrate animal feeding with this group of non-literate women. After much discussion with colleagues, they decided to demonstrate the use of feeding crates in good husbandry by using plastic model animals, such as poultry, cattle and pigs. From their pre-testing, they knew that to make the message clear, the models of the feeding crates had to be three-dimensional. The two development officers experimented for two weeks, using matchsticks and papier mâché to make scaled-down, but realistic, feeding crates. At the workshop for the group, they explained the value of feeding crates, demonstrating how to use them with the plastic animals and the scaled-down matchstick crates. 'The demonstration enabled the women to develop a clear picture of what was needed and why,' says the livestock officer. The remaining workshop time was used to build a life-size feeding crate for a real cow. This session gave the women the motivation and skills to build their own feeding crates when they returned to their village.

Demonstrating a skill or process is an effective way of sharing skills and also allows the trainer to check that the new skill has been successfully learnt.

A simulation is slightly different from a demonstration. The aim of a simulation is to be as close to the real activity as possible. For example, trainee midwives can learn about the dangers of moving a baby's position before birth by using a plastic doll inside a balloon filled with water. The balloon breaks when the trainees try to move the doll, clearly illustrating the teaching point 'do not attempt to change a baby's position before birth'.

In the primary classroom, models and toys can be used to introduce new topics in an interesting way. For example, plastic toys of wild and domestic animals can introduce a lesson on biology or environmental studies. At secondary level, models can be used by the teacher and made by students as part of project work in many subjects including geography, maths, biology and agricultural science.

Always pre-test your models, particularly if you are planning to use them with adult learners, to ensure that trainees are not offended if they perceive them as 'children's toys'.

Rag dolls

Rag dolls can be used to demonstrate how to deliver a baby to students and trainee midwives. However, if you are using children's toys to demonstrate a technique, it is important not to offend those that you are working with: they may feel that you are treating them like children. To avoid this problem, it is essential to pre-test your ideas.

How to make a rag doll baby

You will need

- ticking or other stout material
- graph paper to make a pattern (make your own by drawing a grid of even-sized squares)
- pins
- thread
- kapok or waste cotton for stuffing
- a pair of scissors
- thin rope or twisted cloth

What you need to do

1 Draw a pattern on a piece of graph paper: a circle for the head, sausage shapes for the limbs, oval shape for the body.

2 Pin the pattern onto a folded piece of cloth and cut around it. You will now have two body pieces.

3 Sew the two halves together around the edges and inside out, leaving a small opening at the top of the head, and then turn out the right way.

4 Stuff the doll with kapok or waste cotton and sew up the hole.

5 Make an umbilical cord from thin rope or twisted cloth.

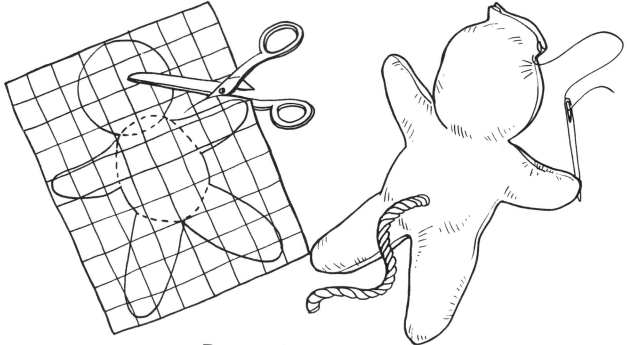

Puppets

A puppet is a small figure representing a person or animal which is moved by various means. Hand puppets are excellent for entertaining an audience. In teaching and development work they are particularly useful for conveying a particular message in a fun and stimulating way.

One of the main advantages of using puppets is that they can say things which (a) may not be considered acceptable for live actors to say in a particular community or (b) children may be reluctant to talk about. The fact that it is the puppet who is speaking creates a useful distance.

❝ Drama, story-telling, singing and dancing are all traditional forms of entertainment in the Solomon Islands. It was therefore a logical choice to include these elements in the health education programme. I'd had no experience of making puppets before and was rather nervous. I sought advice from people who knew more than me...and we plucked up enough courage. We spent a day writing the script (about a sick boy called Daniel) and making some very simple 'stick' puppets from leaves, tree bark, pieces of wood and small fruits. In the evening the veranda of my house became the stage, lavalavas (pieces of brightly-coloured cloth) the curtains and strategically placed hurricane lamps lit the whole show. Despite a few minor disasters – Daniel's head kept falling off, his mother muddled her lines and the curtains were scorched by a faulty kerosene lamp – the show went down well. The puppet operators acted with great verve and enthusiasm and everyone rounded off the evening by exhausting a whole repertoire of songs. Getting started had proved surprisingly easy and introducing puppets to the health education tours turned out to be a popular innovation, although the prototype puppets soon proved unsuitable for travelling and had to be replaced with 'glove' versions made of fabric. The majority of the people had never seen the like before and both adults and children were mesmerised, avidly following each word and action. Asking follow-up questions afterwards gave us the chance to correct any misunderstandings. ❞
Health educator, Solomon Islands

Some puppets can be quick to make, for example, a finger puppet, or they can take several days, for example, a painted papier mâché hand puppet. The following types of puppets will be suitable for the classroom or training sessions. They can also be used to perform a play in front of an audience.

How to make a finger puppet

A finger puppet is placed over one or two fingers. The fingers are moved to make the actions of the puppet.

You will need
▶ a felt-tip pen or biro
▶ a matchbox

What you need to do
1 Draw faces on the tips of the first and second finger. Make them amusing, for example, a happy face or a sad face. You can glue wool on your fingers to make hair if you wish to. You can also decorate the matchbox.

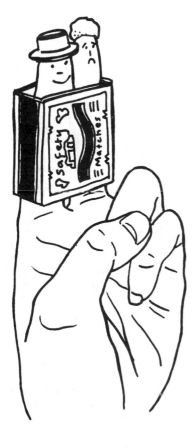

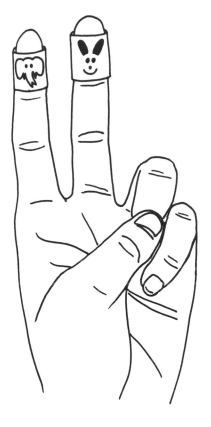

2 Take the inside box out of the matchbox and discard it. Put your fingers up through the outside box. Your fingers are the puppets.

3 Move your fingers around and speak the different parts as you move each finger.

If you do not have a matchbox, you could make a cylinder from a piece of paper and put this around your finger. Draw a face on it and stick hair on the top.

How to use finger puppets

Finger puppets can be used in the classroom to make language practice more fun. They also give students the opportunity to practise the language drill or dialogue on their own or in pairs. The language can then be used as a basis for the students to develop their own stories.

How to make a hand puppet from papier mâché

You will need

▶ papier mâché (see Chapter 6, pages 113–114 for instructions on how to make it)
▶ a mould to support the papier mâché object while it is being made (for example, a balloon, chicken wire, a plastic bottle, a tin can or newspaper rolled up into a ball); you can remove the mould after you have made the object or leave it in
▶ paints
▶ varnish
▶ a brush

What you need to do

1 Build up layers of papier mâché to make the puppet shape. You must allow time for each layer to dry.

2 When all the features have been modelled in papier mâché, paint it. Allow the paint to dry and then add any features using paint. Then give it a final layer of varnish.

3 Make clothes for the puppet.

4 Put your hand up inside puppet's clothes and hold the head. You can also put a hand through one sleeve to make an arm move.

How to use hand puppets

Here are some guidelines for using hand puppets:
- speak loudly and clearly so the audience can hear
- the puppet must face the audience
- move your puppet when it has to speak
- make sure the audience cannot see you
- practise using your own words so that you are fluent
- practise so that all the 'puppets' know the words and when to say them.

Children really enjoyed this teaching method. The training team would give a health lesson, for example, the importance of washing their hands. Then the children would be asked to plan a short play on this theme. The children then put on a puppet show for another group of children.
Environmental health co-ordinator, Sierra Leone

Puppets can be very useful in the field of family planning. People will laugh at them where they couldn't laugh if it was live theatre.
Doctor, Malawi

General guidelines on using puppets

- When you and your students or trainees are making puppets, aim to reflect the local personalities, for example, a mother with a baby on her back, traditional healer and so on. Make sure enough puppets are made.

- If the students or trainees have made the puppets, leave them with the class or group. They may like to create more plays for their own audiences.

- Store the puppets in a solid container (for example, a tea chest or a suitcase) to stop them being crushed. To transport them you could put each puppet in a separate bag.

An enthusiastic art and crafts teacher trainer in Papua New Guinea decided to make puppets with her trainees. She wanted them to put on plays with the primary school students on their next teaching practice.

The trainees were highly motivated and collected local materials and made papier mâché. They then asked the English lecturer for help with writing the plays for the students. They discussed themes and plots and each group wrote a different play.

The trainees took the puppets and the plays to their teaching practice schools. The older students in the schools practised and then performed them for the younger classes. All the plays were very successful. After this the older students asked to make papier mâché puppets themselves. They wrote dialogues and performed them for the other classes. In several schools the plays were performed on open day and were a great success.

6

Basic techniques and materials

This chapter describes some simple design techniques and gives step-by-step instructions for making materials.

All the visual aids described in this book involve some basic design skills, such as lettering and drawing, and in this chapter you will find guidelines which can help you produce an attractive and effective aid. Most of the techniques can be applied to several types of visual aid, so once you have used and mastered a technique, you can apply it to different tasks.

This chapter also gives step-by-step instructions for making some basic materials, such as chalk, glue and papier mâché, using and improvising resources that are available locally.

Chalk

How to make chalk

You will need
▶ chalky earth (This is usually pale-coloured and not very fertile. If you are not sure about what sort of soil is in the area, ask agricultural teachers or local people.)
▶ muslin bag
▶ water
▶ dye (optional)

What you need to do
1 Mix 1 part chalky earth with 4 parts water in a bucket until it reaches a smooth consistency. If you want coloured chalk, add dye to the water. Leave overnight.

2 The next day, pour the water off the soil and water mixture. Then pour the top layer of silt from the mixture. This should be several inches thick. This is your 'chalk'.

3 Put it into a muslin bag and squeeze as much water out of the bag as possible.

4 Hang the bag to drip until the chalk feels like dough mix. Leave overnight.

5 The next day, roll the dough into snake-length pieces. Cut the chalk into desired lengths and leave to dry.

Chalkboard paint

Many school suppliers stock chalkboard paint but if this is unavailable, you can mix matt black paint with powdered chalk to give extra texture. The amount of chalk you need will vary, so you may have to experiment.

Colour

Coloured powdered dyes are available from some shops or T-shirt printers. It is best to choose water-based dyes as these are easier to clean off if you spill them on yourself or your clothes.

You can make coloured dyes yourself by adding a little water to kitchen powders, such as cocoa, instant coffee, paprika, red chilli powder, yellow mustard powder or blue detergent powders.

Dye

Ask local people if any local plants, for example roots, barks, seeds or leaves, can be used as dye colours.

Inks

Mix two parts of alcohol to one part of water and a little powdered dye (blue or black). Stir well.

See also Paint, page 112.

Copying

You can use carbon paper, a banda machine (a simple duplicating machine, often hand-operated), a jelly copier, or a photocopier, or you can go to a print shop to make copies. If you are a teacher, you could draw a design onto a chalkboard, and then ask your class to copy the same design.

Carbon paper

Carbon paper, which can be bought at stationery shops, is a useful way of producing one or more copies. Use a black ballpoint pen and press hard if you are using several layers of carbon paper. The carbon paper should be face-down on the paper you want to transfer the image to. If the carbon slips, secure it with masking tape, a pin or a paper clip.

How to make a jelly copier

You will need
- ▶ one packet of gelatine (11 grams)
- ▶ 50 ml of glycerine
- ▶ two teaspoons of sugar
- ▶ one cup of boiling water
- ▶ a pot
- ▶ a flat baking tray, A4 size or bigger
- ▶ a sponge
- ▶ strong ink – gentian violet, food colouring or overhead projector pens

❛ We made a lot of worksheets on a banda machine. You can buy special A4 banda masters which you write or type on. As long as you clip the carbon original on very securely, bandas can do thirty copies easily – but after that they may start to fade or crease. You can also buy different coloured carbons but this can be expensive and means you spend hours operating the banda. Try to make your writing clear – instead of doing joined-up letters, print words. Many things can go wrong, so it's good to practise. ❜
English teacher, Zanzibar

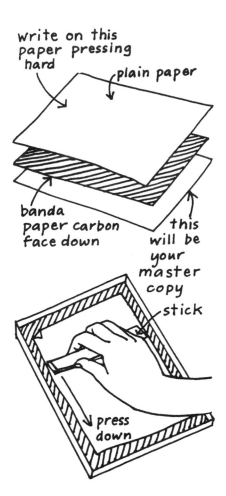

write on this paper pressing hard

plain paper

banda paper carbon face down

this will be your master copy

stick

press down

What you need to do

1 Mix the gelatine and water in a pan. Stir to dissolve.

2 Put the pan on the stove or fire. Add the sugar and let it dissolve. Warm gently.

3 Add the glycerine. Stir well until everything is dissolved. Boil the mixture gently for 1 minute.

4 Remove the mixture from the heat and pour it slowly into the A4 tray. Leave it until the jelly is set.

How to use a jelly copier

1 Make a 'master copy'. Write on good quality paper with a strong ink. (The special paper used for Banda copying is very good for this and can be used with a typewriter.)

2 Put some cold water on a sponge. Wipe the surface of the jelly with the sponge.

3 Place the 'master' face-down. Press it down gently. Leave it for two or three minutes and then peel it off.

4 Place the blank piece of paper you want to print on face-down on the jelly. Smooth it with your hand or a stick. Peel it off immediately. Then repeat with other blank pieces of paper.

5 As soon as you have finished printing, use the sponge and hot water to clean the image off the jelly.

This should make 20 copies.

Photocopying

Black words or lines reproduce the best. Blue pencil marks may not reproduce at all. Try to shut the photocopier lid for the best quality copies. Some photocopying machines overheat if many copies are made, so leave enough time to allow the machine to cool down.

See also Tracing, page 118.

Designs

If you are designing work that will be printed, try to keep it simple. Black and white images work well. Try to avoid tones (shades of grey) because they do not reproduce well.

When you are designing something, remember that some Western artistic conventions may not be understood. For example, cigarette smoke could be mistaken for a spirit, profile drawings may seem as if people are missing limbs. Clothing needs to be drawn carefully. For example, saris may be worn differently by women in the town and in the country.

People will laugh at mistakes, and this will detract from the message. It is important, therefore, to carry out some research first.

Look at local posters and advertising designs to identify what is most effective and most easily understood. Pre-test all your designs before producing the final versions.

Dough

Dough can be moulded to make models in the same way as clay or plasticine. If clayey soil is not available locally, try making your own dough instead.

How to make dough

You will need
- ▶ two cups flour
- ▶ one cup salt
- ▶ one cup water
- ▶ one tablespoon oil
- ▶ two teaspoons cream of tartar
- ▶ dyes for colouring the dough

You can increase the quantity of the ingredients if you want to make a larger amount of dough.

What you need to do

1 Mix the flour, salt, oil and cream of tartar in a pan.

2 Gradually add the water and mix thoroughly to remove any lumps.

3 Cook the dough over a medium heat, stirring all the time.

4 When the dough is stiff, remove the pan from the heat.

5 Remove the dough from the pan, and allow the dough to cool. Wash the pan immediately.

6 When the dough is cool, knead it until it is smooth.

If you want to colour the dough, add dye to the water before you mix it with the flour and salt mixture.

Keep the dough in an air-tight container.

Drawing

How to draw people

For matchstick men and women, use designs from textbooks, development books or magazines. If you practise drawing people, you will find that it is not difficult.

- ▶ Draw a matchstick person first, then fill the limbs out by drawing tubes around them.

Basic shapes of men and women

▶ Alternatively, sketch people using a triangle as a basic shape for men and women.

▶ When drawing adults, make the head and the body the same length as the legs.

▶ Draw the arms straight first. Draw them to come down to below the top of the legs.

▶ Do not draw figures with too much detail, for example with noses, ears and so on.

▶ To draw adults, children and babies in proportion, notice how many times the head fits into the body.

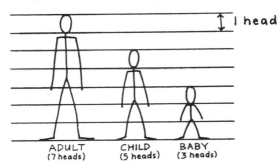

▶ It is a good idea to exaggerate movement when drawing matchstick people.

▶ Join up all the lines of the body. If some lines are not joined, the students may be confused.

▶ Do not draw too much detail during a lesson because the students will get bored.

Faces

1 Draw a circle.

2 Imagine that the circle is divided into three equal parts.

3 Draw the eyes where the first line would be and the mouth where the second line would be. The nose goes in the middle.

Children's faces

1 Divide the face in half. Draw the features on the lower half.

2 Add hair.

If you feel that drawing people is too difficult, cut pictures out of magazines and newspapers instead.

Drawing adults' faces

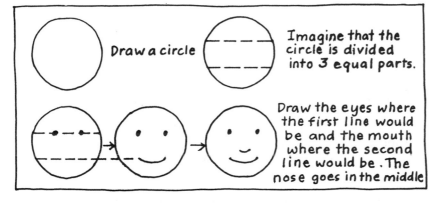

Drawing children's faces

Facial expressions

Facial expressions

happy   very happy   sad   very sad   crying   angry   very angry   tired   nasty

drunk   frightened   sick   surprised

Add hair

man   woman   boy   girl   baby

How to draw objects

I and 2

3 and 4

It is important to keep the drawing simple. For example, to draw a bicycle:

1 Draw a triangle upside down.

2 Draw two circles (wheels) on either side.

3 Draw a line from the centre of one circle to make handlebars.

4 Draw a circle from the centre of the other circle to make a saddle.

How to draw a straight line

There are three ways to draw a straight line on a chalkboard:

1 Draw along the edge of a long piece of wood. Make sure it has a straight edge.

2 Take a piece of string and rub it on one side with a piece of chalk. Ask someone to hold the other end of the string very tightly and level on one side of the chalkboard. Hold the chalk-covered string against the board and flick it. This will leave neat, feint lines. You can then either draw over the feint lines and/or use the lines to write on.

3 You can also take a piece of chalk, and put the point on the board. Keep the chalk on the board and your arm still, and walk slowly across the board, pulling the chalk in a straight line.

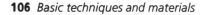

How to draw a circle

1 Put your hand on the board holding a piece of string at the centre of your intended circle.

2 With a piece of chalk in your other hand, move the string to make a circle. Keep the string tight.

This may be easier if you ask someone to help you.

If you want to draw a circle freehand, remember to keep your elbow in the same position all the time. Use your elbow as a pivot. It is a good idea to draw each side of the circle from a different direction.

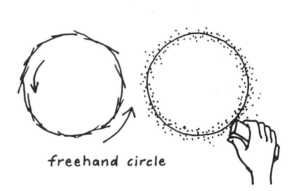

freehand circle

Enlargements

How to make grid enlargements

A small picture can be enlarged, for example to make a flashcard large enough to be used as a poster, using the following method:

1 *Either:* trace (see page 118) the picture you want to enlarge onto squared graph paper, *or* make your own grid. Do this by ruling evenly-spaced vertical and horizontal lines with a pencil across a piece of drawing paper and noting how many lines you needed to draw.

2 Number the grid 1,2,3 and so on, along both the vertical and horizontal axes.

Alternatively, fold the paper in even spaced lines (vertically and horizontally) remembering the number of times you folded the paper.

3 Now make a larger grid with the same number of evenly-spaced squares as the first grid. The squares in this grid will be larger.

4 With a pencil, make dots in the squares of the large grid which correspond to the key lines of your original picture in the smaller grid. This gives you the correct proportions for the enlarged figure.

5 Join the dots to produce the enlarged picture.

How to make rubber band enlargements

1 Knot a small and large rubber band together.

2 Hook one end of the small rubber band to a drawing pin and attach it to the drawing surface.

3 Place your original picture so that its left edge is lined up underneath the knot. The rubber band should be tight.

4 At the other end of the large rubber band, insert a pencil.

5 Hold the pencil firmly (and vertically) in the rubber band. Make the knot follow the outlines of the picture. The pencil will produce an enlarged picture.

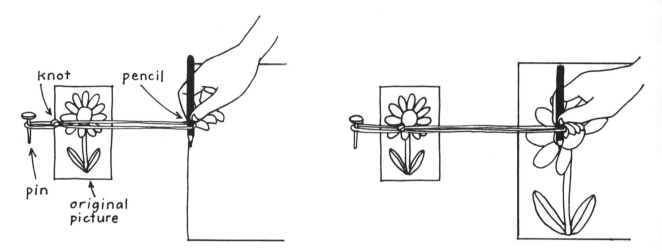

A pantograph is a mechanical device which can be used to enlarge or reduce pictures. You can make your own from scrap materials.

How to make pantograph enlargements

1 Fix point A to the drawing surface.

2 Insert a pencil in point C.

3 Place point B on the original drawing.

4 Hold the pencil firmly and follow the outline of the original drawing with B. The pencil will produce an enlarged drawing.

Points D and E are adjustable so that larger or smaller drawings can be made. You can practise adjusting these points to see the different sizes you can produce.

Glue

There are two ways to make glue (also called starch paste).

How to make glue using flour

This glue is used in the making of papier mâché.

You will need
► half a cup of sifted plain flour (wheat/cassava)
► one cup of water

What you need to do
1 Mix the flour with a little of the water to form a smooth paste.

2 Add the remaining water. Cook the flour and water together, stirring until the flour dissolves.

3 Allow to cool.

How to make glue using rice

You will need
► a handful of rice
► water

What you need to do
1 Cook a handful of rice in water until the rice becomes sticky.

2 Turn off the heat. Keep the rice covered until it is cool.

3 Drain off the water. Use the sticky rice as glue.

Rice glue works well if you need to pin up pictures, for example, on a display board. You may have to press the sticky rice hard to make it stick.

Lettering

You will need to use clear lettering for all your visual aids, including chalkboards, wall displays, banners, posters, newsletters, comic story books and photo stories.

How to write clearly

When you are writing on a chalkboard, stand 40 cm away from the board. Your arm should be very slightly bent, and your elbow and wrist should barely move. Your shoulder should control the movement of the chalk. You may find it useful to draw horizontal chalk lines on the board, so that it is easier to write in a straight line (see How to draw a straight line, page 106). Stand back to make sure that your writing looks clear.

Wherever you are writing, your writing should be the same in style and size. There should be the same spacing between words and lines. The writing should be clear enough to be read from a distance.

The rules of good lettering are:
► All the vertical lines in letters must be parallel.
► The height of all upper case letters should be the same.
► The height of all lower case letters should be the same.
► Plan what you are going to write, to make sure it will fit the space available.

> *From all that I've seen and read, and through experience in my own work, I know that text is much easier to read if it is in upper and lower case letters. The words seem to flow and that makes it easier to read.*
>
> *Graphic artist, Namibia*

It is best to use lower case and upper case letters (capitals), rather than upper case letters only. This is especially important when you are working with people who are not confident readers.

If your work is to be copied on a banda machine, do not use joined-up writing because it can be hard to read.

If you are using a computer to produce work for a newsletter, for example, choose a serif face, which is the easiest type to read. The letters in a serif face have tails. The letters in a sans serif face do not. A popular serif face is Times or Times New Roman.

This is an example of a serif face.
This is an example of a sans serif face.

A fine-nibbed Rotring pen with Indian ink is best for lettering. If you do not have one, use any good pen with black ink. If the ink is not dark enough, it will not reproduce properly.

Letter stencils

A letter stencil is useful to ensure that you use neat, even-shaped letters. Ready-made stencils are easily available. You can also make your own, following the instructions below.

You will need
- ► strong card, cardboard or lino
- ► scissors and/or a sharp knife
- ► a pencil

What you need to do

For upper case letters, you can make one stencil to produce every letter of the alphabet.

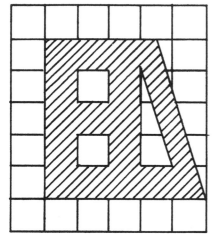

1 Draw the grid on the left on card and cut out the shaded shape. Make sure that the letters will be the size that you want.

2 Use the diagram below as a guide to form each capital letter you need from the stencil. You will need to turn the stencil over to form M, V, W, X and Z.

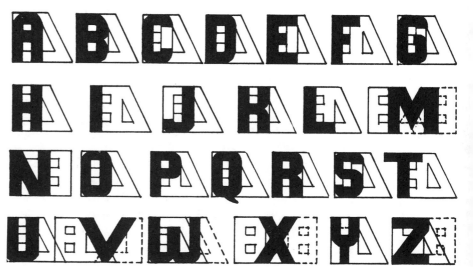

For lower case letters, you will need to make a stencil that gives all the letters of the alphabet individually.

1 Use the template below as a guide. Draw the lower case numbers on card at the size you want. If you want them the same size, you can trace them.

a b c d e f g h i
j k l m n o p q r
s t u v w x y z

2 Cut them out using a sharp knife. You will need to leave small strips of card to connect the middle of some letters to the rest of the template, for example 'o'.

3 Draw around the inside of each shape to create the words that you want to use.

Remember that the upper case letters have to be larger than the lower case letters.

When you have drawn the words you need, you can colour the letters using crayons, marker pens or paint.

Measuring

Good ways of measuring without a tape measure or ruler include a length of string with knots tied at regular intervals, and pre-cut and measured lengths of straight stick.

Originals

If you anticipate using an original (whether it is a picture, photograph, or template), it is important to label clearly who (or which group) it belongs to. Keep it flat in a safe, dry place. A lockable cupboard may be useful.

If you are using originals regularly, keep them in a place that is safe and to which you have easy access. A large stiffened A4 envelope is good for storing paper A4 originals.

Paint

Use purpose-made paint brushes and select the right size brush – small for delicate work, fatter for filling in colours. Otherwise use pieces of cloth or your fingers. Powdered poster paint, which has to be mixed with water, is excellent for children to use because it is easy to wash off. Acrylic and oil-based paints are more expensive and can be hard to clean off hands or clothes. You need to use turpentine to clean the brushes used for oil-based paints. Otherwise they will become stiff and difficult to use. All brushes need to be cleaned immediately after painting has finished.

Powder paints should be kept in a dry, air-tight container. Keep the lids on paints to avoid accidental spillage and to prevent paint 'skins' forming.

How to make powder paint with earth

You will need
- ► sifted earth
- ► cassava starch

What you need to do
To make paint for flesh-coloured puppets, mix sifted earth with some cassava starch. This makes a smooth brown colour. For paler tones, add chalk. For darker tones, add crumbled charcoal.

How to make paint with corn starch

You will need
- ► one heaped tablespoon corn starch
- ► water
- ► one tablespoon detergent or soap
- ► dyes

What you need to do
1 Mix the corn starch with water to form a paste.

2 Add a cup of boiling water.

3 Stir vigorously to avoid lumps.

4 Simmer the mixture until thick and smooth.

5 Add the detergent or soap.

6 Add dye, as required.

How to mix shades

Use small amounts of paints to develop the right shade. Even small amounts of paint cover a large surface, so if you mix too much there may be wastage.

Paper

Paper objects should always be treated carefully. They can be damaged by folding, crumpling, direct sunlight, rain and time. Some pests, for example termites, may eat paper products like manuals and handbooks. To avoid this, keep book storage areas clean and use insect spray.

Where to find large sheets of paper

If you are having problems finding large pieces of paper, try asking for butcher's paper or newsprint. Both are cheap and are readily available in most countries. Brown butcher's paper is available at butcher's shops and newsprint can be found at newspaper offices. You could also try asking local businesses to donate unwanted computer printouts. Used paper flour sacks or cement sacks can be cut up and laid flat for use.

Standard paper sizes

It is useful to know the standard paper sizes:

A2 420 × 594 mm (standard poster size, often used for flipcharts)

A3 297 × 420 mm (half the size of A2)

A4 210 × 297 mm (the most commonly used size of paper, half the size of A3)

A5 148 × 210 mm (half the size of A4)

Papier mâché

Papier mâché is useful for making models, particularly puppets. There are two ways to make papier mâché:
▶ the strip method
▶ the pulp method

How to make papier mâché using the strip method

This is the most common method.

You will need
▶ paper torn into small strips (newspapers or magazines are good for this)
▶ glue (made from flour and water, see page 108)
▶ a mould in the shape of the model you wish to make (such as a balloon, a shape made from chicken wire or crumbled newspaper)
▶ paintbrush

What you need to do

1 Use the paintbrush to paste the strips of paper.

2 Stick the pieces of paper over the mould. Slowly build the shape you want using layers of paper and glue. Alternatively, you could dip the strips of paper in the glue.

3 Allow the model to dry.

4 Repeat steps 2 and 3 two or three times, until the model is the required size.

5 Leave the model to dry completely.

When the model is dry, you can paint and varnish it. You will probably need two coats of paint to cover newspaper. Add the fine details using paint and then one coat of varnish. Allow each coat of paint to dry before applying the next coat.

How to make papier mâché using the pulp method

You will need
- ▶ paper torn into small pieces
- ▶ glue (made from flour and water, see page 108)
- ▶ water
- ▶ two bowls, buckets or similar containers

What you need to do

1 Put the pieces of paper into a bucket or a bowl and pour water over them. Allow the paper to soak in the water for several hours.

2 Squeeze the water out of the paper so that the paper becomes pulp.

3 Put the paper in a second bowl and add the glue to it. Mix it well.

4 Slowly add water. Squeeze the paper until the mixture feels sticky.

5 The mixture can now be moulded into any shape, such as the head of a puppet. You can mould it like clay or plasticine, or you can cover a mould with it.

6 Leave the model to dry completely.

The model can be painted and varnished.

Printmaking

How to make prints using hard vegetables

You will need
- ▶ a hard vegetable, such as a potato or a sweet potato
- ▶ a sharp knife

- ▶ poster paints
- ▶ paper or card

What you need to do

1 Cut off the end of a potato. Then cut a shape into the flat surface with a sharp knife. To make a spotty design, for example, scoop out holes with a large nail or the closed end of a pair of scissors.

2 Put some poster paint onto a plate and allow it to spread out, or spread it with a brush.

3 Dip the cut end of the vegetable into the paint and then press it evenly onto a piece of paper.

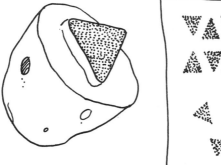

How to make block prints

A printing block can be used over and over again. If you plan to put letters on your block remember that the design will print the opposite way from the one you cut out. Use a mirror and a newspaper to see how the letters should look back to front. You can also use a mirror to check your design before you print it.

You will need
- ▶ a small block of wood, about 16 cm × 16 cm
- ▶ a pencil
- ▶ cardboard
- ▶ paints
- ▶ scissors
- ▶ glue
- ▶ paper or card
- ▶ newspaper

What you need to do

1 Draw a design on a piece of thick cardboard. Remember to draw it back to front.

2 Cut out the shape in one piece and glue onto the block of wood. Wait for the glue to dry.

3 Pour some paint into a tray. Press the block into the paint evenly.

4 Put newspaper underneath the paper to avoid paint going through. Press the block onto the piece of paper.

How to make cotton reel prints

These are useful for making continuous decorative patterns.

You will need
- ▶ an empty cotton reel
- ▶ two pencils or sticks
- ▶ plasticine
- ▶ paints
- ▶ paper or card

What you need to do

1 Push a pencil or a stick through the hole in the centre of the cotton reel.

2 Cover the cotton reel in an even layer of plasticine.

3 Make a pattern in the plasticine using a pencil, or a stick.

4 Roll the cotton reel in paint and then push it across the paper. This will make a continuous decorative pattern.

5 If you want to use another colour, wash the paint off the plasticine with soap and water, and start again.

How to make a print using an empty toilet roll

You will need
- ▶ an empty toilet roll, or other cardboard roll
- ▶ card
- ▶ a pencil
- ▶ glue or sticky tape
- ▶ a piece of thin sponge
- ▶ scissors
- ▶ a thin stick slightly longer than the tube
- ▶ paints
- ▶ paper

What you need to do

1 Stand the empty toilet roll upright on a piece of card. Draw around the end of the roll to make two circles.

2 Cut these circles out and then make a small hole in the centre of each.

3 Glue or tape one circle to each end of the toilet roll tube. Leave to dry.

4 Cut the sponge to the same length as the tube. Roll the sponge around the tube and glue the edges of the sponge together. Do not glue the sponge to the tube or you will not be able to wash it.

5 Make your design by cutting shapes in the sponge with a pair of scissors.

6 Push a thin stick through the holes at the ends of the tube.

7 Pour some paint into a tray. Roll the toilet roll roller in the paint.

8 Then push it across a sheet of paper.

Templates

It is useful to prepare a series of templates for pictures that you need to draw frequently. For example, if you are teaching geography you can make a template map of the country the students are studying.

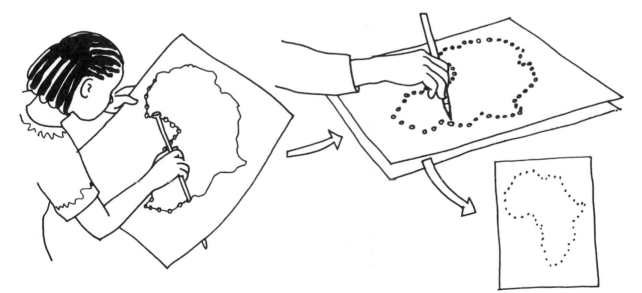

How to make a template

You will need

▶ paper, cardboard or heavy card (from cartons, packets, sacks, brown paper bags) or thin plastic from containers, such as vegetable oil bottles

▶ a leather punch or a knitting needle

What you need to do

1 Make the drawing or shape on heavy card or brown paper.

2 Use a leather punch or a knitting needle to make small holes along the outline of the drawing. This outline is the template.

How to use a template

1 Hold the template against a sheet of paper, for example a flipchart.

2 Make pencil marks in the holes.

3 Take away the template and there will be a series of pencil marks. Join the marks to make a clear outline of the picture.

If you are using the template on a chalkboard, pat a dusty chalk cloth along the holes. When you remove the template there will be a dotted chalky outline of the image. Join the dots with a bold chalk line to make a clear picture.

Tracing

This is a useful method of copying a picture and also for changing a picture. For example, if you are teaching or working with Muslim communities, you could change a picture flashcard showing a village scene with pigs to make a new outline of a village without pigs. This would then be an appropriate teaching tool for that particular community.

How to make a tracing

You will need
- a sheet of thin paper (that you can see through), greaseproof paper or tracing paper
- a soft-leaded pencil (2B is better than HB)

What you need to do

1 Put a sheet of thin paper over the design you want to copy.

2 Using the pencil, trace the image with a heavy line. For extra clarity, go over the line again.

3 Turn the tracing paper over, face down on the surface you want to copy onto. Retrace the lines on the reverse side of the tracing paper to transfer the desired image onto the blank piece of paper or material. Note that this image is the reverse of the original image.

Another way of tracing is to tape the desired design to the inside of a window. Place a sheet of paper over the image and trace it onto the new piece of paper. This technique works best when the sun is shining in through the window.

Useful contacts

The organisations listed below can provide free catalogues or other material, or can be contacted for advice. The list should provide a starting point in your search for ideas, images and assistance.

The organisations are listed by continent and country. The list is by no means exhaustive, but by contacting one organisation in the country in which you work, you will probably find out about others.

Within developing countries it is worth approaching the local offices of international NGOs such as the Save the Children Fund or Oxfam, as well as national NGOs. UN organisations, government ministries, travel agencies, tourist bureaux, airline offices and embassies are also potential sources of books, visual aids, newspapers, magazines and posters. Commercial outlets are often good sources of free supplies for making visual aids.

Visual aids are used abundantly in development education and awareness-raising in the UK and other countries of the North, so, when requesting advice and resources, explain the country and situation you are working in. Visual aids designed for use in the North are not usually appropriate for use in developing countries.

There is also a growing amount of literature concerning participatory approaches and methods, and in many countries a participatory approaches network has been established: contact addresses are supplied below.

International

British Council
The British Council has offices in major cities all over the world, usually with a library attached.

UNICEF
There are UNICEF offices in the capitals of many countries. Look in your local telephone book to find your nearest contact. UNICEF is mainly concerned with long-term development programmes relating to children's needs, encompassing health care, nutrition, disability, water and sanitation, primary and vocational education. It produces publications, some of which are free. UNICEF offices stock and develop visual aids to support their programmes.

Africa

Egypt
Appropriate Communication Techniques (ACT), 22 II Shaheed Yusri Fahmi Street, Ard II Golf, Heliopolis, Cairo. ACT is an Egyptian non-profit making organisation whose aim is to establish and run a resource and training centre for communication skills for development. ACT runs courses for women's groups in health and income-generation in poor areas in Cairo.

Center for Development Services (CDS), 4 Ahmed Pasha Street, Garden City, Cairo.

The Center uses visual aids extensively in its work to support self-determined and self-sustaining change in Egypt. Its programmes involve small businesses, management, agriculture extension, environmental and community health services.

Ethiopia
Farm AFRICA, PO Box 5746, Addis Ababa.

Farm AFRICA is an agricultural NGO experimenting with participatory appraisal methods.

Kenya
AFROLIT, PO Box 72511, Nairobi.

AFROLIT is an adult literacy agency which also publishes material.

Maturity Video Visual, PO Box 14740, Nairobi.

Maturity Video Visual produces and uses films and videos.

Participatory Methodology Forum of Kenya (PAMFORK), PO Box 58684, Nairobi, Kenya. Tel: +254-2-447382. Fax: +254-2-442136.

PAMFORK is a PRA network interested in sharing information about participatory methodologies.

Mozambique
The World Bank Resident Mission, Caixa Postal 4053, Maputo. Tel: +258-1-492841/51/61/71. Fax: +258-1-492893.

Contact for participatory approaches network in Mozambique.

Namibia
The Ford Foundation, PO Box 20614, Windhoek. Tel: +264-61-239133. Fax: +264-61-239060.

Contact for participatory approaches network in Namibia.

North East Health Directorate Health Education Unit, Private Bag 2094, Rundu, Okavango. Tel: +264-(0)67372-426. Fax: +264-(0)67372-371.

This unit trains local secondary students and young people to develop and produce health education materials, including a newsletter and picture stories used by health workers to start discussions with communities about their health problems.

Nigeria

KARATU, 1 Gomwalk Boulevard, Jos, Plateau State. Postal address: PO Box 10353, Jos, Plateau State.

Karatu is a team of teachers based in Jos, Nigeria. Karatu means 'reading' in Hausa. The Karatu team conducts participatory workshops for teachers, empowering them to teach their pupils to read. They also write reading books and train teacher trainers. They are interested in working with any organisation concerned with reading, personal development and community development.

Training Materials Department, International Institute of Tropical Agriculture (IITA), Oyo Road, PMB 5320, Ibadan. Tel: +234-2-241-2626 or 2169. Fax: +234-2-874-2276.

IITA produces a wide range of agricultural visual aids for use in extension which are disseminated throughout Sub-Saharan Africa.

South Africa

Midnet PRA Interest Group, PO Box 101045, Scottsville, Pietermaritzburg 3209. Tel: +27-331-457607. Fax: +27-331-455106.

Contact for participatory approaches techniques.

National Rural Development Forum, PO Box 32434, Braamfontein 2017. Tel: +27-11-3395412. Fax: +27-11-3391440.

Contact for participatory approaches techniques.

Planned Parenthood Association of South Africa (PPASA), 31 Plantation Road, Ackland Park, Johannesburg 2092. PO Box 8687, Johannesburg 2000. Tel: +27-11 482-4601. Fax: +27-11 482-4602.

PPASA is an independent organisation working for planned parenthood, reproductive health and responsible sexuality, primarily with the youth and young adults of South Africa. PPASA produce educational materials for schools, informal settlements and rural areas.

Uganda

Institute for Teacher Education, Department of Teacher Education and Extension, PO Box 1, Kyambogo.

STEPU (Science and Technology Equipment Production Unit), PO Box 7002, Kampala.

Zimbabwe

Foundation for Education with Production/Mambo Press, PO Box 779, Gweru. Tel: +263-(0)154-4016/7. Fax: +263-(0)154-51991.

Asia

Bangladesh

Bangladesh Rural Advancement Committee (BRAC), 66 Mohakhali C/A, Dhaka 1212.

This large national NGO uses visual aids and participatory training in all areas of development and is increasingly using participatory techniques in fieldwork.

Swiss Development Corporation (SDC), House B31, Road 18, Banani, Dhaka.

Contact for those interested in participatory methods.

Cambodia

Cambodia British Centre (CBC), 26 Street 122, Phnom Penh. Tel: 23705/27541.

This is a resource centre developed by the Centre for British Teachers (CfBT) which has an English teacher training project in Cambodia. It contains a sophisticated collection of ELT materials – books, tapes, videos, etc.

Cambodia Development Resource Institute (CDRI), 56 Street 318, Toul Kork, Phnom Penh. Tel: 26103/66094/68053.

CDRI runs training courses in English, Khmer, computing, basic accounting and other topics for local NGOs. There is a well-stocked resource centre full of up-to-date and archive material about Cambodia.

Co-operation Committee for Cambodia (CCC), 35 Street 178, Phnom Penh. Tel: 26009.

CCC is an umbrella organisation co-ordinating and representing the interests of local and international NGOs working in Cambodia. There is a small resource centre containing reports written by NGOs, background papers, books, articles, etc. CCC is an ideal place to find out about other organisations in Cambodia which produce materials.

Population Services International (PSI), 47 Street 302, Phnom Penh. Tel: 62518.

PSI is a non-profit organisation dedicated to the eradication of AIDS. Their work involves AIDS/HIV awareness education and marketing cheap but good quality condoms. They have t-shirts, a human-sized marketing device called CondomMan and other materials about AIDS/HIV.

India

ActionAid India, 3 Resthouse Road, Bangalore 560 001. Tel: +91-80-558-6682. Fax: +91-80-558-6284.

ActionAid uses PRA approaches widely in its development programmes and is now piloting the use of PRA in adult literacy learning. The India office is the contact point for a participatory approaches network.

Aga Khan Rural Support Programme (AKRSP), Choice Premises, Swastik Cross Road, Navrangpura, Ahmedabad 380 009.

AKRSP does a lot of participatory techniques work including training.

The Centre for Health Education Training and Nutrition Awareness (CHETNA), Drive-in Cinema Building, Thaltej Road, Ahmedabad – 380 054, Gujarat.

This NGO develops and adapts materials including child-to-child readers. CHETNA networks and runs training courses. It works with poor women and children.

MYRADA, 2 Service Road, Domlur Layout, Bangalore 560 071.

Among other activities this NGO is adapting PRA methods to the south Indian context and publishes a series of papers on participatory methods. It has made a video on participatory approaches and conducts training.

Tamil Nadu Resource Team (TNRT), Kalanjium, 59A1 Chenglavarayan Street, Madras 600 012, Tamil Nadu. Tel: +91-44-613620. Fax: +91-44-4821897.

A useful contact for those interested in participatory methods.

Indonesia

Driya Media, Jl. Makmur 16, Bandung 40181, PO Box 6715. Tel: +62-22-84614. Fax: +62-22-211282.

Driya Media produces all kinds of visual aids ranging from posters about AIDS/HIV to booklets on VSO Indonesia. They are used extensively by NGOs in Indonesia to produce visual aids for training courses on a variety of issues including health, agriculture, gender and environment.

World Education, Jalan Tebet Dalam IV F/75, Jakarta 12810. Tel/fax: +62-21-8291026.

World Education uses participatory methods in adult learning and working with communities. As an initial contact for participatory techniques practitioners it can pass enquiries to others.

Nepal

Basic and Primary Education Project (BPEP), Keshar Mahal, PO Box 422, Kathmandu. Tel: 419393. BPEP Curriculum Centre, Sanothimi, Kathmandu. Tel: +977-1-610572.

BPEP is a government project with long involvement in non-formal education. The Curriculum Centre produces a wide range of literacy materials.

Innovative Forum for Community Development (IFCD), Babar Mahal, PO Box 518, Kathmandu. Tel: +977-1-228158.

IFCD developed the idea of post-literacy materials and established a newsletter to co-ordinate NGO activities.

Participatory Natural Resources Management Programme, International Centre for Integrated Mountain Development, GPO Box 3226, Kathmandu. Tel: +977-1-525313. Fax: +977-1-524509.

Interested in participatory approaches in mountain regions of India, Pakistan, China, Bangladesh, Burma and Afghanistan.

Secondary Education Development Project (SEDP), Sanothimi, Kathmandu. Tel: +977-1-610172.

A government project which devises its own materials

and manuals for use by teacher trainers in secondary schools.

Society for Participatory and Cultural Education (SPACE), Chakupat, Patan Dhoka, PO Box 1668, Kathmandu. Tel: +977-1-523774.

This NGO has diverse programmes which vary by region and the specific needs of the ethnic groups with which they work. Most of their work is with non-literate women and they develop their own material.

United Missions to Nepal (UMN), Thapathali, PO Box 126, Kathmandu. Tel: +977-1-2288118/228060.

UMN has wide-ranging activities including a series of 100 readers entitled 'Piper Series'. The series uses Language Experience Method, collecting real-life stories of people living within the project areas.

World Education, Kamal Pokhari, PO Box 937, Kathmandu. Tel: +977-1-415790.

World Education provides technical assistance to the Ministry of Education's adult literacy programmes, producing post-literacy materials.

Pakistan

Adult Basic Education Society (ABES), 6 Empress Road, Lahore – 54000.

English Language Resources Unit (ELRU), Aga Khan Education Services, House No. 3&4, F-17/B, KDA Scheme V, Off Khayaban-e-Iqbal, (Behind English Book House), Kehkashaan, Clifton, Karachi – 75600.

ELRU produces materials to support teachers of English.

Teachers' Resource Centre (TRC), 67–B Garden Road, Karachi.

TRC produces a range of materials to support their teachers' training and development work.

Health Education Resource Centre (HERC), GPO 504, 84E Rehman Babar Road, Peshawar, NWFP.

HERC's team of Afghan artists produce a wide variety of visual aids. HERC is particularly noted for its screen printing for health and mine awareness programmes.

Sri Lanka

Intercooperation, 92/2 D.S Senayaka Mawatha, Colombo 8. Tel/fax: +94-1-691215.

Participatory approaches network contact.

Vietnam

Jaako Poyry AB, PO Box 36, Hanoi. Tel: +84-211148. Fax: +84-211798.

Participatory approaches network contact.

Europe

United Kingdom

ActionAid, Hamlyn House, Macdonald Road, London N19 5PG, UK. Tel: +44-(0)171-281-4101. Fax: +44-(0)171-272-0899 (main number) or +44-(0)171-281-5146 for enquiries about educational publications.

ActionAid is doing some very interesting work using PRA in integrated rural development (Pakistan) and literacy (El Salvador) among others. There is an RRA network in India. Contact the relevant desk officers for further information or visit in-country offices.

Agricultural Extension and Rural Development Department (AERDD), 3 Earley Gate, The University, Whiteknights Road, Reading RG6 2AL. Tel: +44-(0)118-931-8119. Fax: +44-(0)118-926-1244.

AERDD runs a number of post-graduate courses. Communications as they relate to extension, education and rural development form one of the main areas of teaching. Its documentation centre contains material on visual aids and communications in development and visits can be arranged. It publishes the Rural Extension Bulletin three times a year which summarises practical experiences of implementing rural development programmes and projects. Correspondence about subscriptions should be addressed to the Editor, The Rural Extension Bulletin, at the address above.

Alternative Health Technology Action Group (AHRTAG), Farringdon Point, 29–35 Farringdon Road, London EC1M 3JB. Tel: +44-(0)171-242-0606. Fax: +44-(0)171-242-0041.

AHRTAG shares information about primary health care and promotes the development of low cost and appropriate technologies for health. If you are working in a developing country you can receive their newsletters free of charge. These include AIDS Action and Child Health News. Other publications may also be free of charge to those working in developing countries. AHRTAG has a resource centre and information service and can refer you to an extensive list of newsletters available to development workers. It is best to make an appointment to visit.

Book Aid International, 2 Coldharbour Place, 39/41 Coldharbour Lane, Camberwell, London SE5 9NR. Tel: +44-(0)171-733-3577. Fax: +44-(0)171-978-8006.

Book Aid International (formerly Ranfurly Library Service) sends out books to developing countries free of charge. It is best to write with details of the kind of books you need. Book Aid will then send you more information about the scheme and a project proposal and book requirements form. You need to complete and return these forms before books can be sent to you. Please note that they usually only send to schools and other educational institutions, and to national libraries.

Child-to-Child Trust, Institute of Education, 20 Bedford Way, London WC1H 0AL. Tel: +44-(0)171-612-6650. Fax: +44-(0)171-612-6645.

The child-to-child programme promotes the idea that children can be the most effective communicators. Children of school age can be taught and encouraged to take an interest in the health and welfare of other children, whether younger siblings or those who do not attend school. You can see their publications at the Institute of Child Health or make an appointment to visit the Child-to-Child Trust. A publication list is available (also from the Institute of Child Health and TALC) which includes resource books and readers. Some activity sheets and readers are available in Spanish (from TALC), Arabic (from ARC, PO Box 7380, Nicosia, Cyprus) and French (from EDICEF, 26 rue des Fosses Saint-Jacques, 75005 Paris, France).

Communication Therapy International (CTI), 25 Hilbre Road, Burnage, Manchester M19 2PU.

CTI is concerned with people in less developed countries who have communication disorders. Membership is open to anyone who wishes to share and learn from their experiences. CTI holds study days and produces a resource pack, which costs £4.00, and a newsletter.

Commonwealth Institute, Kensington High Street, London W8 6NQ. Tel: +44-(0)171-602-7374. Fax: +44-(0)171-603-4535.

The Commonwealth Institute has materials on communication methods relating to health, and on multi-cultural education. Permanent country displays show the artistic and decorative heritage of Commonwealth countries.

Health Images, Holly Tree Farm, Walpole, Halesworth, Suffolk IP19 9AB. Tel: +44-(0)1986-784402.

A group of illustrators and artists whose activities focus on the training of community-level workers in making and using pictures to support processes of empowerment. Their basic aim is to help improve the availability of visual materials for health and development communication in developing countries.

Institute of Child Health, University of London, 30 Guilford Street, London WC1N 1EE. Tel: +44-(0)171-242-9789. Fax: +44-(0)171-831-0488.

The Institute has a large resource centre with full-time staff to help you find what you need (Tel: 0171 242 8698). It stocks TALC and a range of health-related publications.

Institute of Development Studies (IDS), Brighton, Sussex. Tel: +44-(0)1273-678269. Fax: +44-(0)1273-691647/621202.

Members of IDS have been pioneers in the development and implementation of RRA and PRA approaches. Further information and a catalogue of publications is available from the publications department.

Intermediate Technology Publications, 103–105 Southampton Row, London WC1B 4HH. Tel: +44-(0)171-436-9761. Fax: +44-(0)171-436-2013.

This is the publishing arm of Intermediate Technology Development Group which aims to enable poor people in the developing world to develop and use technologies which give them more control over their lives and which contribute to the long-term development of their communities. The IT Bookshop, at the same address, stocks a broad range of books on appropriate technology and development. IT's excellent annual catalogue, Books By Post, is available at the bookshop or by post. The sections on Education, Training and Communication Skills; and Audio-visual Aids list some useful publications.

International Institute for Environment and Development (IIED), Sustainable Agriculture Programme, 3 Endsleigh Street, London WC1H 0DD. Tel: +44-(0)171-388-2117. Fax: +44-(0)171-388-2826.

IIED does both policy research and grassroots work around the world. The sustainable agriculture programme is a leading exponent of Participatory Rural Appraisal and produces a catalogue listing reports, monographs, booklets and books on the subject. It also publishes *PLA (Participatory Learning and Action) Notes.* This copyright-free series shares information and experiences from the field. There is no charge to subscribers from the South and back copies are available.

International Planned Parenthood Federation (IPPF), Regent's College, Inner Circle, Regents Park, London NW1 4NS. Tel: +44-(0)171-486-0741. Fax: +44-(0)171-487-7950.

The world's largest non-governmental organisation working in the field of planned parenthood and related health services. IPPF produces films and slides on family planning and contraception. You can make an appointment to visit the library.

Oxfam, 274 Banbury Road, Oxford OX2 7DZ. Tel: +44-(0)1865-31311. Oxfam Publications, PO Box 120, Oxford OX2 7FA. Tel: +44-(0)1865-313196. Fax: +44-(0)1865-313117.

Oxfam works with poor people regardless of race or religion in their struggle against hunger, disease, exploitation and poverty in Africa, Asia, Latin America and the Middle East through relief, development and research overseas, and public education at home. To find out about visual aids for development purposes you should contact the relevant desk officer or the in-country office. Oxfam is also using PRA methods. Oxfam Publications publishes and distributes books and other resource materials as part of Oxfam's education and information programme in the UK and abroad. A free catalogue is produced yearly.

Scottish Education and Action for Development (SEAD), 23 Castle Street, Edinburgh EH2 3DN. Tel: +44-(0)131-225-6550.

Scottish Environmental Education Council, University of Stirling, Stirling FK9 4LA. Tel: +44-(0)1786-467868.

Sustainable Farming Systems, Agriculture Building, West Mains Road, Edinburgh EH9 3JG. Tel: +44-(0)131-667-1041.

Teaching Aids At Low Cost (TALC), PO Box 49, St Albans, Hertfordshire, AL1 4AX, UK. Tel: +44-(0)1727-853869. Fax: +44-(0)1727-846852.

TALC supplies teaching aids and books for use by health care workers but some of its publications are useful for many skill areas. Write for TALC's mail order catalogue, which is updated each year. The Institute of Child Health and the IT Bookshop both sell TALC books, slide sets and other visual aids.

World Association for Christian Communication (WACC), 357 Kennington Lane, London SE11 3QY. Tel: +44-(0)171-582-9139. Fax: +44-(0)171-735-0340.

WACC has a library of reference material on visual aids with an emphasis on mass media which you can visit by appointment. It publishes the quarterly journal *Media Development.*

World Wide Fund for Nature (WWF UK), Education Department, Panda House, Weyside Park, Godalming, Surrey GU7 1XR. Tel: +44-(0)1483-426444. Fax: +44-(0)1483-424609.

Contact WWF UK for details of its educational programmes and for its free and very comprehensive publications catalogue.

The Netherlands

Centre for the Study of Education in Developing Countries (CESO), Kortenaerkade 11, PO Box 29777, 2502 LT The Hague. Tel: +31-(0)70-426-0291. Fax: +31-70-426 0299.

CESO has a library which contains much 'grey literature' (unpublished documents, field reports, etc.), as well as some audio-visual aids. Catalogues of documents available in the library can be ordered. It is CESO's policy to make the documentation and database available to users worldwide and to distribute publications free of charge to people working in developing countries.

Transfer of Technology for Development (TOOL), Sarphatistraat 650, 1018 AV Amsterdam. Tel: +31-20-6264409. Fax: +31-20-6277489.

TOOL is a non-profit organisation directed towards technology transfer to and between developing countries. TOOL has two departments. The Reference Centre contains a documentation centre, a bookshop, a publishing unit and a 'question and answer' service. You can send off for a free publications catalogue and order by post. The Consultancy department works with local organisations to develop technological innovations. TOOL links up interested parties through a multi-functional e-mail network called TOOLNET.

North America

United States of America

Educational Materials Unit Program for International Training in Health (INTRAH), 208 N. Columbia Street, Chapel Hill, North Carolina, N.C. 27514.

World Neighbors, 5116 North Portland, Oklahoma City, OK 73112. Tel: +1-405-752-9700.

This organisation makes available the film strips and slides produced by and with the rural communities it works with. World Neighbors publishes a newsletter, *Soundings,* on rural communications.

Canada

International Development Research Centre (IDRC), Communications Division, PO Box 8500, Ottawa, Ontario KIG 3H9. Tel: +1-613-236-6163. Fax: +1-613-563-0815.

IDRC produces films and videos on community health, water and sanitation and agriculture. Its free catalogue is available in English, French and Spanish.

Pacific

Fiji

Director of Extension Services, University of the South Pacific, PO Box 1168, Suva.

A large range of distance learning and support materials for students who undertake university courses through extension centres throughout the Pacific Islands.

Health Education Unit, Ministry of Health, PO Box 2223, Government Buildings, Suva.

The Unit produces a range of health education materials in the three official languages in Fiji: Fijian, Fiji Hindi and English.

National Food and Nutrition Committee, PO Box 2450, Government Guildings, Suva.

An organisation campaigning for better nutrition and related issues – produces reports, posters and other materials.

Pacific Concerns Resources Centre, Private Mail Bag, Suva.

One of the few NGOS owned and run by Pacific islanders. Campaigns on a range of regional issues such as nuclear testing. Produces a monthly magazine and other resources.

Tonga

Curriculum Development Unit, PO Box 61, Nuku'alofa.

Produces appropriate materials for use in schools, including textbooks and resource materials.

Vanuatu

Wan Smolbag Theatre, PO Box 404, Port Vila.

A theatre group that uses plays, cultural items and workshops to convey important health, social, educational, environmental and human development messages at grass roots level. Helps other theatre groups in the region.

South America

Bolivia

Co-ordinator of Research and Development Programs (DPIP), Universidad Nur, Ave. Banzer No. 100, Casilla 3273, Santa Cruz. Tel: +591-3-363939. Fax: +591-3-331850.

Participatory approaches network contact.

Mexico

Programa de manejo participativo de recursos naturales del Grupo de Estudios mbientales, A.C., Allende 7 Sta. Ursula Coapa, D.F. CP 04650. Tel/fax: +52-5-6171657 (in Mexico City).

Participatory approaches network contact.

Acknowledgements

The authors would like to thank all the VSO volunteers and their colleagues, VSO staff and everyone who generously helped produce material, ideas and inspiration for this book, in particular: Andrew Baird, Silke Bernau, Wendy Bower-Paintsil, Su Braden, Amanda Brook, Andy Byers, David Burslem, Fiona Campbell, Megan Cartin, Pete Chaffey, Caroline Cheyne, Christine Cooke, Pia Cossu, Linda Cracknell, Louise Cummins, Louise Dempsey, Angela Ellins, Ingrid Emsden, Sally Etherton, Sam Featherston, Brendan Foley, Victoria Francis, Brian Goddard, Hugh Govan, Alan Greenwood, Trudi Gurling, Gail Handley, Arne Heineman, Ainé Holderness, Andy Inglis, Eleanor Kercher, Julian Lewis, Bob Linney, Kenny McArthur, Linda Mages, Sarah Murray Bradley, Pat Norrish, Ruth Nussbaum, Gail Paterson, Martin Taylor, Jeremy Trayner, Tara Winterton.

The authors and publishers are grateful for permission to reproduce the following illustrations: the poster on page 45 from *Orbit*, VSO's quarterly magazine, Issue 46; the Community Forestry Monitoring charts on page 46 from *Participatory Monitoring and Evaluation – A handbook for training field workers*, FAO, Bangkok, 1988; the postcard 'Women Weaving the World Together' on page 47 from an original by courtesy of Khemara, Cambodia; the cartoon on page 60 by Gladys Agar from *Orbit*, VSO's quarterly magazine, Issue 45; the illustration of the photo story on page 65 is based on 'Leilei's Dilemma', produced by the Save Project, SCF Australia, in the Solomon Islands; the graph on page 71, the pie charts on page 73, and the women's and men's maps on page 75 are reproduced from *PLA Notes* 22, February 1995, produced by the Sustainable Agriculture Programme, IIED; the rainfall calendar on page 82 and the crop calendar on page 83 are reproduced from *Rapid Rural Appraisal – A closer look at rural life in Wollo*, 1988, Sustainable Agriculture Programme, IIED/Ethiopian Red Cross Society; the time trend calendar on page 86 is reproduced from *An Introduction to Rapid Rural Appraisal for Agricultural Development*, 1988, Sustainable Agriculture Programme, IIED; the illustration of a flow chart on page 87 is based upon an original in *A Guide to Basic Book Production*, Book 1, by Judith Wilkinson, 1985; The British Council/ITP; the rubber band and pantograph enlargements on page 108 and the universal stencil on page 110 are reproduced by courtesy of the International Planned Parenthood Federation.

Index

VSO Books

VSO Books is the publishing unit of Voluntary Service Overseas. More than 21,000 skilled volunteers have worked alongside national colleagues in over 60 countries throughout the developing world since 1958. VSO Books draws upon this range of experience to produce publications which aim to be of direct, practical use in development. Care is taken to present each area of volunteer experience in the context of current thinking about development.

A wide readership will find VSO Books publications useful, ranging from development workers, project implementers and teachers to project planners, policy-makers and ministry officials in both the South and the North.

Information from VSO Books can also be found on the World Wide Web:
http://www.oneworld.org/vso/

Other books in the VSO/ Heinemann Teachers' Guide series

The Maths Teachers' Handbook by Jane Portman and Jeremy Richardson, 128pp, paperback, VSO/Heinemann, ISBN 0 435 923188

This book is a vital resource for maths teachers in developing countries who are asked to deliver a mainly academic syllabus to large classes with few resources. This handbook contains practical activities and teaching tips for topics common to a range of syllabi, including guidance on the cultural context of mathematics and teaching pupils whose first language is not English.

The Science Teachers' Handbook by Andy Byers, Ann Childs, Chris Lainé, 128pp, paperback, VSO/Heinemann, ISBN 0 435 92302 1

The Science Teachers' Handbook is full of exciting and practical ideas for demonstrating science in even the lowest-resourced classroom. VSO teachers and their colleagues from around the world have developed these ideas to bring science to life using local resources and creativity.

Setting Up and Running a School Library by Nicola Baird, 138pp, paperback, VSO/Heinemann, ISBN 0 435 92304 8

This lively and practical guide makes running a school library easy and fun. This book has been written especially for non-librarians and because it is based on the work of VSO teachers and their colleagues in low-resource situations, it takes into account the reality of schools in developing countries. Even with few resources it is possible to set up a school library which will make a real difference.

Current VSO Books publications include:

Adult Literacy – A handbook for development workers by Paul Fordham, Deryn Holland and Juliet Millican, 170pp, paperback, VSO/Oxfam Publications, ISBN 0 85598 315 9

Agriculture and Natural Resources – A manual for development workers by Penelope Amerena, 117pp, hardback looseleaf, VSO, ISBN 0 9509050 3 8

Care and Safe Use of Hospital Equipment by Muriel Skeet and David Fear, 188pp, spiral bound, VSO Books, ISBN 0 9509050 5 4

Culture, Cash and Housing – Community and tradition in low-income housing by Maurice Mitchell and Andy Bevan, 134pp, paperback, VSO/ITP, ISBN 1 85339 153 0

Introductory Technology – A resource book by Adrian Owens, 134pp, paperback, VSO/ITP, ISBN 1 85339 064 X

Made in Africa – Learning from carpentry hand-tool projects by Janet Leek, Andrew Scott and Matthew Taylor, 70pp, paperback, VSO/ITP, ISBN 1853392146

Participatory Forestry – The process of change in India and Nepal by Mary Hobley, 360pp, paperback, VSO/ODI, ISBN 0 85003 204 0

Using Technical Skills in Community Development – An analysis of VSO's experience by Jonathan Dawson, ed Mog Ball, 55pp, paperback, VSO/ITP, ISBN 1 85339 078 X

Water Supplies for Rural Communities by Colin and Mog Ball, 56pp, paperback, VSO/ITP, ISBN 1 85339 112 3

For more information about VSO Books, contact:

VSO Books
317 Putney Bridge Road
London SW15 2PN
UK
Tel: (+44) (0) 181 780 2266
Fax: (+44) (0) 181 780 1326
e-mail: sbernau@vso.org.uk